IMPROVING SURVEY QUESTIONS

Design and Evaluation

Floyd J. Fowler, Jr.

**Applied Social Research Methods Series
Volume 38**

SAGE Publications
International Educational and Professional Publisher
Thousand Oaks   London   New Delhi

For information address:

 SAGE Publications, Inc.
2455 Teller Road
Thousand Oaks, California 91320
E-mail: order@sagepub.com

SAGE Publications Ltd.
6 Bonhill Street
London EC2A 4PU
United Kingdom

SAGE Publications India Pvt. Ltd.
M-32 Market
Greater Kailash I
New Delhi 110 048 India

Printed in the United States of America

Library of Congress Cataloging-in-Publication Data

Fowler, Floyd J.
    Improving survey questions: design and evaluation / Floyd J.
Fowler, Jr.
        p.   cm. — (Applied social research methods series; v. 38)
    Includes bibliographical references and index.
    ISBN 0-8039-4582-5 (cloth: alk. paper). — ISBN 0-8039-4583-3
(pbk.: alk. paper)
        1. Social surveys—Methodology.   2. Social sciences—Research—
Methodology.   I. Title.   II. Series.
HN29.F67   1995
300′.723—dc20   95-16861

This book is printed on acid-free paper.

95 96 97 98 99 10 9 8 7 6 5 4 3 2 1

Sage Project Editor: Susan McElroy

IMPROVING SURVEY QUESTIONS

Applied Social Research Methods Series
Volume 38

APPLIED SOCIAL RESEARCH METHODS SERIES

Contents

Preface

I believe that the design and evaluation of survey questions is the most fertile current methodological area for improving survey research. Poor question design is pervasive, and improving question design is one of the easiest, most cost-effective steps that can be taken to improve the quality of survey data.

An important origin of this book was a project that I worked on with Charles F. Cannell of the University of Michigan, exploring alternative ways to pretest survey questions. In that study, we selected a sample of questions used in major government and academic surveys to be the focus for our evaluation efforts. Although it was not our main purpose to assess the quality of current survey questions, an incidental finding was that a significant portion of the questions used by well-regarded survey organizations did not meet minimum standards. It is apparent to me that the field of survey research can do better than current practice. The past decade has seen significant growth in studies of question design, as well as advances in techniques for question evaluation. Although this is still very much work in progress, there are numerous well-grounded principles about how to design and evaluate questions, and those are the subject of this book.

One special challenge for improving survey questions is that people with all manner of backgrounds, and no special training, write survey questions—politicians, lawyers, economists, accountants, and journalists, to name just a few. Everyone thinks he or she can write good survey questions. So, the book is intended for anyone who wants to write survey questions, as well as all those who want to use the results from a survey; neither statistical issues nor social science jargon should get in the way of any reasonably well-educated person being able to read and appreciate the messages herein.

Foremost among these, almost certainly, is the emphasis on question evaluation. Without doubt, Chapter 5, which deals with presurvey question evaluation, is the most important chapter in the book. At the moment, for most survey organizations, the evaluation of survey questions is pretty rudimentary. I believe that if the protocols outlined in Chapter 5 became routine in survey research, the quality of survey research would go up immeasurably. Thus, if I have a primary hope for this book, it is that it plays a part in increasing the extent to which questions are evaluated before they are used in surveys.

JACK FOWLER

1

Questions as Measures: An Overview

WHAT IS A GOOD QUESTION?

In the social sciences, and increasingly in medical sciences as well, important measurements are based on a question-and-answer process. Children answer questions in standardized tests, and the results are used as measures of their intelligence; the unemployment rate is a calculation of answers about employment status and desire to be in the workforce; studies of medical outcomes rely on patients' answers to questions about their health status and quality of life.

There is an almost limitless body of desirable and useful information that can be gathered only by asking people questions. In some cases, that is because we want to know facts that are difficult to observe systematically. For example, although some crimes are reported to police, many are not. The best way to estimate the rate at which people are victims of crime is to ask a sample of people about their victimization experiences. We also are often interested in measuring phenomena that only individuals themselves can perceive: what people think or know, or what they feel.

Obviously, questions and answers are part of everyday conversation; they are part of the fabric of our social life. However, the distinctive focus of this book is how to turn an everyday process into rigorous measurement.

There are several implications of the notion that the answers to questions will be used as measures. First, we are not interested in the answers for their own sake. Rather, we are interested in what the answers tell us about something else. As a result, one critical standard for a good question-and-answer process is that it produces answers that provide meaningful information about what we are trying to describe.

1

Second, the purpose of measurements usually is to produce comparable information about many people or events. Hence, it is important that the measurement process, when applied repeatedly, produces consistent results.

These points lead to the beginning of the answer to, "What is a good question?" A good question is one that produces answers that are reliable and valid measures of something we want to describe.

Reliability is used in the classic psychometric sense of the extent to which answers are consistent: when the state of what is being described is consistent, the answers are consistent as well (Nunnally, 1978). Validity, in turn, is the extent to which answers correspond to some hypothetical "true value" of what we are trying to describe or measure (Cronbach & Meehl, 1955).

Each year, political campaigns, newspapers, marketing organizations, governments, and university scholars commission surveys that lead to collecting data from hundreds of thousands of people. These surveys are done by mail, by telephone, and by personal interview. They cover virtually every topic imaginable. Although there are several potential sources of error in survey data, the validity of results of these surveys depends critically on the design of the questions that are asked. Regardless of the mode of data collection or the subject matter, there are some common standards for questions and some common principles about how to meet those standards. Although the primary focus of this book is on the design of questions for population surveys, the book articulates general principles that apply whenever questions are used to provide systematic information about any group of people or events.

CHARACTERISTICS OF QUESTIONS AND ANSWERS THAT AFFECT MEASUREMENT

When thinking about whether or not a question is a good measure, it is necessary to consider the question itself, its form and wording, and the kinds of answers the question is designed to evoke.

One standard for a good question is that all the people answering it should understand it in a consistent way and in a way that is consistent with what the researcher expected it to mean. The fact that respondents can differ from the researchers and from one another in how they use and understand language makes this one of the most difficult standards to reach. However, the extent to which it is achieved is critical to the quality of the resulting measurement.

Second, a good question must be able to be administered in a consistent way. Questions are presented to people in written form or by having an interviewer read them. If the question is presented in writing, the standard is that all respondents should be able to read the question. If the question is to be administered by an interviewer, the standard is that interviewers can and will read the question the way it is written.

A third standard for a good question is that it consistently communicates to all respondents the *kind* of answers that are wanted and are acceptable. To the extent that respondents differ in their perception of what constitutes an adequate answer, their answers will differ for reasons that have nothing to do with what we are trying to measure.

Question: When did you move to Kansas City?
Possible answers:
In 1948.
When I was 10.
After I left college.

All of those answers are possible and reasonable, because that question does not provide a clue about what kind of answer to give. "When did you move to Kansas City?" is not a good question. "In what year did you move to Kansas City?" is a better question, because it specifies the kind of answer that is wanted.

Another criterion for questions is the extent to which respondents are able to answer them. In some cases, of course, whether or not people can answer the questions is actually the information that is being sought—for example, when researchers are trying to measure knowledge or ability. When the goal is not to measure the knowledge of the respondents, it constitutes a source of error in measurement if people are asked questions to which they do not know the answers.

Finally, we should ask questions to which respondents are *willing* to give correct and valid answers. To the extent that some respondents purposefully distort their answers, the validity of measurement is reduced.

So, there are five basic characteristics of questions and answers that are fundamental to a good measurement process:

1. Questions need to be consistently understood.
2. Questions need to be consistently administered or communicated to respondents.
3. What constitutes an adequate answer should be consistently communicated.
4. Unless measuring knowledge is the goal of the question, all respondents should have access to the information needed to answer the question accurately.
5. Respondents must be willing to provide the answers called for in the question.

There is a history in survey research of thinking of question design as an art, not a science (e.g., Payne, 1951). A key difference between art and science is that in art, goodness is in the eye of the beholder. In science, there are consistent standards for "goodness." In this case, the ultimate standards for goodness are the validity and reliability with which a question produces answers that measure something. Over the past few decades, the above generalizations have evolved about characteristics of questions needed to provide valid data. Moreover, we have been learning more about how to apply those generalizations to the design of individual questions. This book describes what we now know about how to design questions that meet the standards outlined above.

QUESTION EVALUATION

Although there are some generalizations about how to design good questions, a critical part of the science of survey research is the empirical evaluation of survey questions. Like measurement in all sciences, the quality of measurement in survey research varies. Good science entails attempting to minimize error and taking steps to measure the remaining error so that we know how good our data are and we can continue to improve our methods.

There are two types of question evaluation: those aimed at evaluating how well questions we propose to ask meet the five standards above, which can be thought of as process standards, and those aimed at assessing the validity of answers that result.

In order to assess the extent to which questions meet process standards, there are a number of possible steps that can be taken. These include:

1. Focus group discussions
2. Cognitive interviews, in which people's comprehension of questions and how they go about answering questions is probed and evaluated.
3. Field pretests under realistic conditions.

Each of these activities has strengths and limitations in terms of the kinds of information that they provide about questions. However, in the last decade there has been a growing appreciation of the importance of evaluating questions before using them in a research project, and a great deal has been learned about how to use these techniques to provide systematic information about questions.

There also is a set of evaluative strategies to find out how well answers to questions produce valid measurements. These include:

1. Analysis of resulting data to evaluate the strength of predictable relationships among answers and with other characteristics of respondents.
2. Comparisons of data from alternatively worded questions asked of comparable samples.
3. Comparison of answers against records.
4. Measuring the consistency of answers of the same respondents at two points in time.

If the answers to a particular question constitute a valid measure, there usually are predictable ways in which they should be associated with the answers to other questions or with known characteristics of respondents. Analyses can be done to provide evidence that the answers constitute measures of what the researcher was trying to measure.

The other strategies for evaluation outlined above require special-purpose data collection efforts that would not typically be part of a survey. However, they provide additional, very important ways of evaluating the extent to which there is error in survey measurement. If two forms of the same question are asked of the same samples, or comparable samples, the distribution of answers should be the same if measurement is error free. To the extent that answers to two comparable questions do not produce the same results, there is error in one or both of the results from those questions.

It is not common to check answers from a survey against records or some other standard. When such studies have been done, most often samples are drawn of people for whom records are available, such as those who have been hospitalized. The people then are interviewed about those events, and the survey answers are compared with the data from records. Of course, records contain errors too, so differences between survey responses and records are not unequivocal indicators of survey error. Despite that limitation and the fact that such studies tend to be expensive and, hence, relatively rare, many important methodological advances have resulted from record-check studies.

Finally, reinterviewing a sample of respondents, asking the same questions twice and comparing the results, can provide useful information about the validity and reliability of answers. The results, too, are not definitive. If the true answers could change, inconsistencies cannot be interpreted unequivocally as errors of measurement. However, when questions pertain to situations or events unlikely to change between the two data collections, differences in answers to the same question can be inferred to imply error (though consistency over time does not ensure that either answer is correct).

Each of these approaches can provide valuable evidence about the quality of measurement, and studies using these techniques are an important part of advancing the science of collecting good data by asking questions.

ORGANIZATION OF THE BOOK

The goal of the book is to teach readers what we currently know about how to design good questions and how to evaluate them.

One critical distinction is between questions designed to measure factual or objective data and those designed to measure subjective states. There are some questions that lie in a murky area between subjective and objective. For example, when people are asked to rate their health, whether the answers are taken as measures of the respondents' actual health status or their perceptions of health may lie in the eye of the investigator. Nonetheless, many questions are aimed at ascertaining undeniably objective events, such as visits to doctors or whether or not a person is employed, whereas others are aimed at undeniably subjective states, such as perceptions, attitudes, and opinions. For objective questions, the notion of validity in theory, if not in practice, is the correspondence between a survey report and some other measure of the same phenomenon. In contrast, there is no way to evaluate the reporting of a subjective state, independent of a person's own reports. Because the question goals differ, as well as the criteria for evaluating their validity, the discussion of these two kinds of questions is separated.

In Chapter 2, what is known about how to write good questions aimed at collecting information about objective facts and events is presented. Chapter 3 addresses generalizations about how to write good questions to measure subjective phenomena. Chapter 4 discusses some alternative ways to attack some common measurement problems.

Chapters 5 and 6 are devoted to techniques for evaluating questions. Chapter 5 describes how to evaluate the extent to which questions are consistently understood and consistently administered, and how to provide tasks that respondents are able and willing to do. Chapter 6 discusses the various ways to evaluate the data resulting from a set of questions.

In the final chapter, Chapter 7, a systematic summary of generalizations is presented about how to design and evaluate questions.

2

Designing Questions
to Gather Factual Data

The focus of this chapter is on how to write questions to collect information about objectively verifiable facts and events. Some such questions ask for descriptions of people: their ages, genders, countries of origin, or marital status. Some such questions ask for reporting of what people have done or what has happened to them: obtaining service from doctors, being a victim of burglary, being laid off from a job, or being arrested for drunk driving. Still another class of topics is what people do or how they lead their lives: how much they exercise, what they have eaten or bought, or how they vote.

Although the range of topics is wide, the common element of all the questions to be discussed in this chapter is that, at least in theory, the information to be provided in the answers could be objectively verified. True, in many cases it would take an omniscient, omnipresent observer to keep track of how many soft drinks a person consumed in the last month or how many days a person spent all or part of the day in bed because of injury or illness. However, the fact that there is an objectively definable set of events or characteristics at issue makes a difference: there are right and wrong answers to these questions. The right answers are those that the omniscient, omnipresent observer would provide. This contrasts with the subject of the next chapter, the measurement of subjective states, for which, indeed, there are no right or wrong answers.

Among questions about objective facts, some are aimed at characterizing people whereas others are aimed at counting or describing events. Sometimes the same question can be used to do both.

For example, when a respondent is asked how many times he or she has been a patient in a hospital overnight or longer in the past year, two kinds of estimates could result. First, one could estimate the total number of hospitalizations experienced by respondents. Second, one could estimate the percentage of respondents who had at least one hospitalization experience during the past year. In the following pages, we are going to be discussing strategies for overcoming problems with questions. Whether a question is aimed at counting events or characterizing people sometimes has a bearing on the optimal solution to a question design problem.

There are five challenges to writing a good question:

1. Defining objectives and specifying the kind of answers needed to meet the objectives of the question.

2. Ensuring that all respondents have a shared, common understanding of the meaning of the question. Specifically, all respondents should have the same understanding of the key terms of the question, and their understanding of those terms should be the same as that intended by the person writing the question.

3. Ensuring that people are asked questions to which they know the answers. Barriers to knowing the answers can take at least three forms:
   a. never having the information needed to answer the question
   b. having the information at some point, but being unable to recall the information accurately or in the detail required by the question
   c. (for those questions that ask about events or experiences during some period of time) difficulty in accurately placing events in time

4. Asking questions that respondents are able to answer in the terms required by the question. It is possible to ask questions to which respondents literally know the answers but are unable to answer the way the investigators want because of a lack of fit between the desires of the investigator and the reality about which the respondent is reporting.

5. Asking questions respondents are willing to answer accurately.

All this must be accomplished with a question that can be administered consistently and has the same meaning to all the people who are going to answer the question so that answers can be aggregated to produce statistical data.

QUESTION OBJECTIVES

One of the hardest tasks for methodologists is to induce researchers, people who want to collect data, to define their objectives. The difference between a question objective and the question itself is a critical distinction. The objective defines the kind of information that is needed. Designing the particular question or questions to achieve the objective is an entirely different step. In fact, this whole book is basically about the process of going from a question objective to a set of words, a question, the answers to which will achieve that objective.

Sometimes the distance between the objective and the question is short:

Objective: Age

Possible Question 2.1: How old were you on your last birthday?

Possible Question 2.1a: On what date were you born?

The answers to either of these questions probably will meet this question objective most of the time. An ambiguity might be whether age is required to the exact year, or whether somehow broad categories, or a rounded number, would suffice. Question 2.1 produces more ages rounded to 0 or 5. Question 2.1a may be less sensitive to answer than Question 2.1 for some people, because it does not require explicitly stating an age. There also may be some difference between the questions in how likely people are to err in their answer, due to recall or miscalculations. However, the relationship between the objective and the information asked for in the questions is close, and the two questions yield similar results.

Objective: Income

Possible Question 2.2: How much money do you make per month on your current job?

Possible Question 2.2a: How much money did you make in the last twelve months from paid jobs?

Possible Question 2.2b: What was the total income for you, and all family members living with you in your home, from jobs and from other sources during the last calendar year?

First, it should be noted that there are imperfections in each of the three questions. However, the key point is that each of those questions is a possible approach to meeting the objective as stated, but the results will be very different. Obviously, current salary or wage rate might be the best measure of the quality or status of the job a person holds. However, if the purpose of measuring income is to find out about the resources available to the person, income for the past year might be a more relevant and appropriate measure. Even more appropriate, because people tend to share in and benefit from income from other family members, the total family income from all people and all sources might have the most to do with how "well off" the person is.

A good question objective has to be more specific than simply "income." More broadly, a question objective can be defined only within the context of an analysis plan, a clear view of how the information will be used to meet a set of overall research objectives. Measuring income is actually a way of measuring social status, resources, or quality of employment. It is necessary to be explicit about the question objective in order to choose a question.

In the course of trying to design and evaluate questions, researchers often are forced to be more specific about their research objectives, what they want to measure and why, than they had been before. Indeed, one of the most common complaints among methodologists who work on question evaluation is that researchers do not have a clear sense of their goals. Until researchers decide what their goals are, it is impossible to write the ideal question.

Another example:

Objective: Soft drink consumption

Possible Question 2.3: How many soft drinks did you drink yesterday?

Possible Question 2.3a: How many soft drinks did you drink in the last seven days?

Again, readers are warned that the above questions both have flaws. However, the issue is the relationship between the question objective and what the specific questions would achieve. One issue is whether the goal is to describe soft drink consumption, to estimate how many soft drinks are consumed by a sample of respondents, or to characterize the respondents in terms of their patterns of soft drink consumption.

For example, the first question will produce a more accurate count of soft drink consumption but for a very limited period. Because behavior on one day is not a very good way to characterize an individual, it would be a poor way to characterize individuals in terms of high, moderate, or low soft drink consumption.

The second question, although likely subject to more response error because it poses a more difficult reporting task, will do a better job than the first of characterizing the individual.

We need a picture of the role of the information in an analysis plan, what the purpose of having the information is, in order to refine the objective and choose a question. If this is a survey for soft drink manufacturers, and the goal is to make a good estimate of aggregate consumption, the questions should be aimed at getting good, precise estimates of total consumption (like Question 2.3). On the other hand, if this is a health survey, and the goal is to identify the extent to which soft drinks are part of people's diets, then characterizing individual patterns of consumption will be the goal (like Question 2.3a).

One more example:

Objective: Use of medical care

Possible Question 2.4: How many times have you seen or talked to a doctor about your health in the past two weeks?

Possible Question 2.4a: How many times have you received any kind of medical care in the last two weeks?

Possible Question 2.4b: How many times have you received any kind of medical care in the last 12 months?

There are many aspects of uncertainty generated by this question objective. Two are illustrated by variations in the questions. One issue is what is meant by medical care. Does it only mean visits to a medical doctor, or are there other kinds of experiences that should count? People receive medical care from nonphysicians such as chiropractors, nurses, physicians' assistants, or physical therapists. Should such care be included, or not? Another ambiguity might be whether services from M.D.s such as psychiatrists or ophthalmologists, that might not seem like "medical care," should be counted.

Another issue is, again, whether the goal is to count events, to get estimates of how much service is being used, or to characterize individuals: is this person a high or low user of medical care services? Collecting information for only a few weeks might be the best way to get a good count of visits to doctors, but it is a poor way to characterize the extent to which a particular individual has been using medical services.

The soundest advice any person beginning to design a survey instrument could receive is to produce a good, detailed list of question objectives and an analysis plan that outlines how the data will be used. An example of such a document is Figure 2.1. Although the level of detail can vary, the creation of a document similar to Figure 2.1 serves at least three critical functions. First, it is an outline for the question design process. It not only specifies the goals of each question; it also helps to identify questions that serve no purpose in a survey instrument. If a researcher cannot match a question with an objective and a role in the analysis plan, the question should not be asked.

Second, by relating proposed questions to an outline of objectives, weaknesses in the specified objectives can be identified.

Finally, by stating the objectives in advance, researchers are reminded that designing questions that people are able and willing to answer is a separate task, distinct from defining research objectives. Figure 2.1 does not specify any questions; it only begins to specify the kind of information the answers to some questions should provide. One of the main origins of terrible survey questions is that the researcher did not make the transition from a question objective to a question; the objective was simply put in question form. The hope was that the respondent would do the work for the researcher and produce information that would meet the objective. That seldom works.

Let us now turn to some of the specific challenges for designing questions that meet research objectives.

DEFINITION OF CONCEPTS AND TERMS

One basic part of having people accurately report factual or objective information is ensuring that all respondents have the same understanding of what is to be reported, so that the researcher is sure that the same definitions have been used across all respondents. This is one of the most difficult tasks for the designer of survey questions, and failure to do it properly is a major source of error in survey research.

For example, respondents were asked how many days in the past week they had any butter to eat. Many people use the terms butter and margarine interchangeably, so respondents were inconsistent in whether they included or excluded margarine when they answered the question. When the question was rewritten to explicitly exclude margarine, 20% fewer people said they had had any "butter" to eat at all in the past week than was the case when the term was left undefined (Fowler, 1992).

Purpose of Survey: Study correlates of use of medical care. We think medical care
is likely to be a function of the following.
    Fiscal resources to afford medical care
    Need for medical care
    Access to medical care
    Perception of value of medical care
Within each of these categories, measurement objectives include:
Fiscal resources relevant to medical care
    Annual family income past year (all sources)
    Liquid assets (savings, bank accounts)
    Health insurance
Need for medical care
    Chronic health conditions that might require care
    Onset of acute illness
    Injuries
    Age/gender (to match with appropriate routine tests and exams)
Access to medical care
    Regular provider or not
    Perceived proximity of provider
    Perceived ease of access
    Perceived financial barriers
Perception of value of medical care
    When not ill (checkups, screening, etc.)
    For chronic conditions (not life-threatening)
    For acute conditions (self-limiting)
Use of medical care
    Visits to doctors
    Other medical services (not M.D.)
    Emergency room use
    Hospitalizations

Figure 2.1. Example of an Outline of Survey Content and Question Objectives

A similar example comes from efforts to measure exercise. The most
common form of exercise for adults in the United States is walking.
However, people are uncertain whether or not to include walking when
they report the amount of exercise they do. Answers to survey questions
about exercise are seriously affected by whether the wording explicitly
includes walking, excludes walking, or leaves the matter undefined.

There are two basic approaches to ensuring consistent understanding
of terms.

1. The researcher can provide complete definitions so that all or most of the
ambiguities about what is called for are resolved.

2. The respondents can be asked to provide all the information needed in order for the researcher to properly classify events for respondents. In other words, rather than trying to communicate complex definitions to all respondents, if adequate information is reported by respondents, complex criteria for counting can be applied consistently during the coding or analysis phase of a project.

Certainly the most common way to write survey questions that are commonly understood is to build needed definitions into the questions.

Example 2.5: In the past week, how many days did you eat any butter?

Problem: There are two potential ambiguities in this question. First, it has already been noted that whether the term "butter" includes margarine or not is ambiguous. Second, sometimes it has been found that "the past week" is ambiguous. It could mean the seven days preceding the date of the interview. It also could mean the most recent period stretching from Monday through Sunday (or Sunday through Saturday).

Possible Solution 2.5a: In the past seven days, not counting any margarine you may have eaten, how many days did you eat any butter?

Comment: The reworded question reduces ambiguity both about whether to include or exclude margarine and about the period that is to be covered.

Example 2.6: How many times have you been hospitalized in the past year?

Comment: Possibly "hospitalized" is a complex term that everyone will not understand. Sometimes people receive services in hospital clinics, and people go to hospitals for day surgery. Do these services count? There also is the potential ambiguity, parallel to the last example, about the reference period. What is the period to which "the past year" refers?

Possible Solution 2.6a: In the past twelve months, since (DATE) a year ago, how many different times have you been admitted to a hospital as a patient overnight or longer?

Comment: The new question clarifies several possible ambiguities, including the fact that each new admission counts as a new hospitalization event, that hospitalization requires that a person be a patient, and that the person must be in the hospital overnight or longer (which, e.g., excludes day surgery events). It also clarifies the reference period.

Sometimes, the definitional problems are too complicated to be solved by simply changing a few words or adding a parenthetical phrase.

Example 2.7: What is your income?

Problem: As discussed above, there are numerous issues about how to calculate income. Among them are whether income is current or for some period of time in the past, whether it is only income earned from salaries and wages or whether it includes income from other sources, and whether it is only the person's own income that is at issue or includes income of others in which the respondent might share.

Example 2.7a: Next we need to get an estimate of the total income for you and family members living with you during 1993. When you calculate income, we would like you to include what you and other family members living with you made from jobs and also any income that you or other family members may have had from other sources, such as rents, welfare payments, social security, pensions, or even interest from stocks, bonds, or savings. So, including income from all sources, for you and for family members living with you, how much was your total family income in 1993?

Comment: That is a very complicated definition. It is necessary because what the researcher wants to measure is a very complicated concept. Even this complex definition avoids, or fails to address, some important issues. For example, what does the respondent do if household composition at the time of the interview is different from during the reference period? The question also does not specify whether take-home pay or total income before deductions is to be reported.

Example 2.8: In the past year, how many times have you seen or talked with a medical doctor or a physician's assistant about your health?

Problems: This question is taken from the National Health Interview Survey and is frequently asked in health surveys. As noted previously, questions about medical care pose numerous problems regarding what should be reported because the definitions are so complicated.

When the rules for counting events are quite complex, providing a comprehensive, complex definition probably is not the right answer. At the extreme, respondents may end up more confused and the results may actually be worse than if definitions were not provided. A different approach is probably needed.

One approach is to add some extra questions to cover commonly omitted kinds of events. For example, in response to the general question about visits to doctors, it has been found that receiving advice over the telephone from a physician, seeing nurses or assistants who work for a physician, and receiving services from physicians who are not always thought of as "medical doctors" often are left out. One solution is to ask a general question, such as Example 2.5 above, and then ask some follow-up questions such as:

Question 2.8a: Other than the visits to doctors that you just mentioned, how many times in the past 12 months have you gotten medical advice from a physician over the telephone?

Question 2.8b: Other than what you've already mentioned, how many times in the past twelve months have you gotten medical services from a psychiatrist?

The same kind of thing can be done with respect to income:

Example 2.9: When you gave me the figure for your total family income, did you include any income you might have had from interest on stocks, bonds, or savings accounts?

Example 2.9a: When you gave me your income figure, did you include all the income that you had from rents?

Example 2.9b: Now, if you add in the kind of income you just mentioned that you did not include initially, what would be your estimate of your total family income in 1993?

Using multiple questions to cover all aspects of what is to be reported, rather than trying to pack everything into a single definition, often is an effective way to simplify the reporting tasks for respondents. It is one of the easiest ways to make sure that commonly omitted types of events are included in the total count that is obtained. However, this approach can be pushed even further, in ways that may make for even better question design strategies.

In some cases, if definitions are very complex, it does not make any sense to try to communicate a shared definition to all respondents. Building on the examples above, instead of trying to communicate to respondents how the researcher wants to define total family income, respondents can be asked a series of questions about the kinds of income they and other family members have had over some period, and what they amounted to. Then the researcher can put together the reported components to fit a particular definition of income that is going to be used for a particular analysis.

There are three rather compelling advantages to such an approach. First, it makes the questions clearer; it is not necessary to communicate a complex, cumbersome definition consistently to all people. Second, it makes the reporting task simpler and more reasonable; the respondent does not have to add income from multiple sources. Third, it may enable the researcher to produce several different measures of income, which may serve different useful analytic purposes. For example, the income of the respondent from earnings might be a good measure of the quality of employment, but the total family income may be a better measure of available resources. Of course, asking multiple questions takes more interviewing time. However, that too may be an advantage. Taking more respondent time, by asking more questions, will improve respondent recall.

If a rough estimate of socioeconomic status is all that is required, a single general question, with all of its flaws, may be acceptable. However, the approach of using multiple questions is often a good alternative to trying to convey complex definitions to respondents.

Example 2.10: What kind of health insurance plan do you have: a staff model health maintenance organization, an IPA, PPO, or unrestricted fee-for-service health plan?

Comment: That may seem to be a ridiculous question; it is unreasonable to think that most people can make these distinctions among health insurance plans. The approach outlined above, of trying to communicate common definitions, would seem unlikely to succeed given the complexity of models of health insurance that exist in the United States. However, there are some questions that people can answer that probably would enable researchers to classify the kind of health insurance plan to which most people belong.

Question 2.10a: In your health plan, can you initially go to any doctor you want, or can you only go to certain doctors or places for your health care?

Question 2.10b: (If from a specific list or group) Do the physicians you see only see people who are part of your plan, or do they see other kinds of patients too?

Question 2.10c: When you receive medical services under your plan, do you yourself always pay the same amount, no matter that the service, or does the amount you pay depend upon the service you receive?

Comment: Maybe the answers to these questions would not enable researchers to make all the distinctions that they would want to make. Moreover, there is a possibility that some people might not be able to answer some of these questions. However, they are much more likely to be able to answer these questions accurately than to learn the definitions of IPA's and HMO's. The general idea of asking people a series of questions they can answer, then attempting to apply more complex definitional strategies to classify patients and their experiences, is a sound way to solve many definitional problems.

Example 2.11: In the past twelve months, were you the victim of a burglary?

Example 2.12: In the past twelve months, were you the victim of a robbery?

These again are examples of questions that have complex, technical definitions. Burglary is the crime of breaking and entering with intent to commit a felony. Robbery is the crime of taking something from someone by force or threat of force. If a person breaks into a home, and the residents are there and are confronted by the intruder, the would-be burglar becomes a robber. It makes no sense to try to communicate these definitions to respondents so that they can say whether they were burglary or robbery victims. Rather, what makes sense is to have people describe the relevant details of events they experienced, then code those events into the proper, detailed criminal categories.

Sometimes this can be done by asking a series of short, specific questions. For example, when the classification hinges on whether or not the intruder was confronted by the residents, it is important to ask that specific question. In other cases, respondents may be allowed to respond in narrative fashion, describing their experiences, which then can be coded into categories using specific definitions and decision rules.

Proper question design means making certain that the researcher and all respondents are using the same definitions when people are classified or when events are counted. In general, researchers have tended to solve the problem by telling respondents what definitions the researchers want to use and then asking respondents to do the classification work. Although sometimes that may be the best way to solve the problem, good question design usually will make the task as simple as possible for respondents. It is a new extra step for most investigators to think about what information they need about people that would enable them to do the classification task. However, if investigators identify what simple, easy questions people can answer that will provide the basis for classification, on many occasions better measurement will occur.

KNOWING AND REMEMBERING

Once a question has been designed so that all respondents understand what is wanted, the next issue is whether or not respondents have the information needed to answer the question. There are three possible sources of problems:

1. The respondent may not have the information needed to answer the question.
2. The respondent may once have known the information but have difficulty recalling it.
3. For questions that require reporting events that occurred in a specific time period, respondents may recall that the events occurred but have difficulty accurately placing them in the time frame called for in the question.

Do Respondents Know the Answers?

Often, the problem of asking people questions to which they do not know the answers is one of respondent selection rather than question design. Many surveys ask a specific member of a household to report information about other household members or about the household as a whole. When such designs are chosen, a critical issue is whether or not the information required is usually known to other household members or to the person who will be doing the reporting.

There is a large literature comparing self-reporting with proxy reporting (Cannell, Marquis, & Laurent, 1977; Clarridge & Massagli, 1989; Moore, 1988; Rodgers & Herzog, 1989). There are occasions when it appears that people can report as well for others as they do for themselves. However, unless questions pertain to relatively public events or characteristics, others will not know the answers. Across all topics, usually self-respondents are better reporters than proxy respondents.

There is another dimension to the topic of knowledge that more directly affects question design. Sometimes respondents have experiences or information related to a question but do not have the information in the form that the researcher wants it. A good example is a medical diagnosis.

There is a literature that shows a lack of correspondence between what conditions patients say they have and what conditions are recorded in medical records (Cannell, Fisher, & Bakker, 1965; Jabine, 1987; Madow, 1967). At least part of this mismatch results from patients not being told how to name their conditions. For example, the patient thinks he has high blood pressure but says he does not have hypertension, because that is not a term he has been given. The patient knows she has growths but did not know the technical name was tumors. It is even easier to think that a physician would not bother to tell a patient that the name for "heart trouble" was "ischemic heart disease." Going back to an example discussed above, there is now a complex array of health plans. Health researchers would like to identify the kind of plans to which people belong, because they are potentially important covariates of the kind of medical care people receive. Respondents are likely not to know the technical terms for the kind of plan to which they belong, even though they have information about the way their plans work that could be used to classify them appropriately.

Having said that, it is common for surveys to ask respondents for information that they do not have. When insurance pays part of the bill, many respondents never know the total cost of the medical services they receive. Many people do not know the medical specialty of the physician that they see. Many people do not know how much their health insurance costs, particularly when a significant portion of it is contributed by their employer.

One critical part of the preliminary work before designing a survey instrument is to find out whether or not the survey includes questions to which some respondents do not know the answers. The limit of survey research is what people are able and willing to report. If a researcher wants to find out something that is not commonly known by respondents, the researcher must find another way to get the information.

Stimulating Recall

Memory researchers tell us that few things, once directly experienced, are forgotten completely. However, the readiness with which information and experiences can be retrieved follow some fairly well-developed principles.

Some memories may be painful and subject to repression. However, that is not the issue for the sorts of things measured in most surveys. Rather, the three principles that probably are most relevant include (Cannell, Marquis, & Laurent, 1977; Eisenhower, Mathiowetz, & Morganstein, 1991):

1. the more recent the event, the more likely it is to be recalled
2. the greater the impact or current salience of the event, the more likely it is to be recalled
3. the more consistent an event was with the way the respondent thinks about things, the more likely it is to be recalled.

How does one obtain accurate reporting in a survey? Obviously, one key issue is what one chooses to ask about. If the researcher wants information about very small events that had minimal impact, it follows that it is not reasonable to expect respondents to report for a very long period. For example, when researchers want reporting about dietary intake or soft drink consumption, it is found that even a 24-hour recall period can produce deterioration and reporting error resulting from recall. When people are asked to report their behavior over a week or two weeks, they resort to giving estimates of their average or typical behavior, rather than trying to remember (Blair & Burton, 1987). If one wants accurate information about consumption, reporting for a very short period, such as a day, or even keeping a diary are probably the only reasonable ways to get reasonably accurate answers (A. F. Smith, 1991).

This same kind of trade-off between accuracy of reporting and the length of time about which someone is reporting is a constant in survey design. The National Crime Survey, conducted by the Bureau of the Census for the Department of Justice, and the National Health Interview Survey both initially asked for one year reporting of crimes and hospitalizations respectively. However, there was such a drop-off in the accuracy of reporting of events that occurred more than six months before the interview that the surveys now use only events reported within six months of an interview as a basis for generating estimates of the quantity of those events. Indeed, the National Health Interview Survey reports the number of visits to doctors and the number of days people lose from work based on reporting for only the two weeks prior to the interview, because of concerns about inaccuracy of reporting for longer periods (Cannell, Marquis, & Laurent, 1977; Lehnen & Skogan, 1981).

A defining characteristic of most interviews is that they are quick question-and-answer experiences. The level of motivation of respondents varies, but for the most part a survey is not an important event in respondents' lives. Hence, without special prodding, respondents are unlikely to invest a significant amount of effort in trying to reconstruct or recall the things that the survey asks them to report (Cannell, Marquis, & Laurent, 1977). For these reasons, researchers have explored strategies for improving the quality of the recall performance of respondents.

One of the simplest ways to stimulate recall and reporting is to ask a long, rather than a short, question. This does not mean making questions more complex or convoluted. However, adding some introductory material that prepares the respondent for the question has been shown to improve reporting (Cannell & Marquis, 1972). One reason may be simply that longer questions give respondents time to search their memories.

Two more direct strategies are used to improve recall. First, asking multiple questions improves the probability that an event will be recalled and reported (Cannell, Marquis, & Laurent, 1977; Sudman & Bradburn, 1982). Second, stimulating associations likely to be tied to what the respondent is supposed to report, activating the cognitive and intellectual network in which a memory is likely to be embedded, is likely to improve recall as well (Eisenhower et al., 1991). The two approaches are interrelated.

Asking multiple questions can be an effective way of improving recall for three different reasons. First, and most obviously, asking close to the same question more than once is a way of inducing the respondent to "try again." Every time a respondent dives into his or her memory bank, the chances of coming up with an answer are improved. Also, one of the effects of asking multiple questions may be to increase the level of motivation of the respondent, and thereby to increase the amount of dedication with which the respondent tries to perform the task of recall.

Second, a specific way of asking additional questions is to focus on the kinds of events that are particularly likely to be forgotten. For example, one-day stays in the hospital are underreported at a much higher rate than other hospital admissions (Cannell & Fowler, 1965). Specifically asking respondents whether or not they have had a one-day stay (for example, in connection with a false labor) may trigger a slightly different approach to searching and lead to recall of events that were otherwise forgotten.

Third, additional questions can focus on some of the possible consequences of events to be reported, which in turn may trigger recall. For example, if one has been a victim of a crime, it is likely that the police were called or an insurance claim was filed. Asking about calling police or filing claims may trigger recall of a crime.

In a parallel way, recall of medical services received may be stimulated by asking about consequences of such medical services such as buying medications, filing insurance claims, missing work because of illness, or having to make child care arrangements.

There are limits to what people are able to recall. If a question calls for information that most people cannot recall easily, the data will almost certainly suffer. However, even when the recall task is comparatively simple for most people, if getting an accurate count is important, asking multiple questions and developing questions that trigger associations that may aid recall are both effective strategies for improving the quality of the data.

The above has been mainly focused on dealing with not recalling events that should have been reported. Equally important is the problem of overreporting. For example, suppose we ask people whether or not they voted in the last election. The most common response error in response to that question is overreporting, people reporting that they voted when in fact they did not (Sudman & Bradburn, 1982). Part of the reason (discussed in detail later in the chapter) is that voting is seen by some as a socially desirable behavior, so they are motivated to recall and report voting. In addition, however, getting people to remember *not* doing something is a particularly formidable challenge.

Psychologists have theorized that one way to improve the accuracy of reporting is to ask respondents to recreate an experience in their minds. For example, with respect to voting, it might be important to remind respondents who the candidates were and what other issues were on the ballot. Preliminary questions could ask respondents to report where they vote, whether or not they have to get off work to vote, how they are transported to the voting place, and the like. By taking respondents through a series of steps likely to be involved in doing something, the odds of triggering a key memory are increased, and the chances become increasingly good that the respondent will be able to reproduce the experience more accurately.

Placing Events in Time

Many of the issues discussed above could reflect an interrelationship between recalling the event at all and placing it in time. If a survey is to be used to estimate the annual number of hospitalizations for a particular sample, people are asked what essentially is a two-part question: Have you been in the hospital recently, and how many times were you in the hospital in exactly the last twelve months?

Studies of recall and reporting behavior show that many of the problems with survey data about such topics stem from difficulties in placing events properly in the time frame designated by the researchers. One of the reasons that hospitalizations that occurred ten to twelve months before an interview are particularly poorly reported is that, in addition to difficulty remembering whether or not the hospitalization occurred at all, respondents have difficulty remembering whether a hospitalization actually occurred before or after that arbitrary line of twelve months ago.

It does not matter a great deal whether the reference period is one week, one month, or one year. If a survey estimate depends critically on placing events in a time period, it invariably is a problem.

There are two approaches researchers use to try to improve how well respondents place events in time:

1. They stimulate recall activities on the part of respondents to help them place events in time;
2. They design data collection procedures that generate boundaries for reporting periods.

In order to improve the ability of respondents to place events in time, the simplest step is simply to show respondents a calendar with the reference period outlined. In addition, respondents can be asked to recall what was going on and what kind of things were happening in their lives at the time of the boundary of the reporting period. Filling in any life events, such as birthdays, can help to make the dates on the calendar more meaningful. If respondents are supposed to report events in the past year, respondents can be asked to think about what they were doing a year ago: where they were living, what was going on in the family, what they were doing at work. If they are able to conjure up some events that they can associate with the date on or about a year before the interview, or that constitute a clearly definable point in time, it may make it easier for them to decide whether crimes or hospitalizations occurred before or after that point (e.g., Sudman, Finn, & Lannon, 1984).

A related strategy is to ask people to do some associating to improve their perception of the dates or times of year that certain events occurred. So, if respondents are being asked about crimes that occurred to them, they may be asked to think about what the weather was like, what they were wearing, or what else was going on in their lives, which may enable them to come closer to figuring out the approximate date when an event occurred.

These strategies are somewhat time consuming in an interview setting. They often require some individualized efforts on the part of interviewers that are not easy to standardize. As a result, relatively few surveys actually use these techniques. In addition, it probably is fair to say that although some of these techniques seem to improve reporting marginally, none seems to be a major breakthrough.

A very different approach to improving the reporting of events in a time period is to actually create a boundary for respondents by conducting two or more interviews (Neter & Waksberg, 1964). During an initial interview, respondents are told that they are going to be asked about events and situations that happen during the period prior to the next interview. The subsequent interview then asks people about what has happened between the time of the initial interview and the time of the second interview.

Such designs have three helpful characteristics. First, they do produce a clear time boundary. Although the initial interview may not be a big event in people's lives, it does have some cognitive significance for respondents. Second, in their first interview respondents usually are asked to report recent events of the sort to be counted. Researchers then are able to check events reported in the second interview against those reported in the initial interview. If there is double reporting, that is, telescoping events from before interview #1 into the period covered in interview #2, it can be identified. Third, the fact that respondents are alerted to the fact that they will be interviewed about certain sorts of events makes them more attentive and therefore better reporters.

Obviously such reinterview designs are much more expensive to implement than one-time surveys. However, when accurate reporting of events in time is very important, they provide a strategy that improves the quality of data.

Finally, giving respondents a diary to keep should be mentioned. There are special challenges to getting people to maintain diaries. However, to obtain detailed information, such as food consumption or small expenditures, for a short period of time, diaries are an option that should be considered (Sudman & Bradburn, 1982; Sudman & Ferber, 1971).

THE FORM OF THE ANSWER

Most questions specify a form the answers are supposed to take. The form of the answer must fit the answer the respondent has to give.

Example 2.13: In the past 30 days, were you able to climb a flight of stairs with no difficulty, with some difficulty, or were you not able to climb stairs at all?

Comment: This question imposes an assumption: that the respondent's situation was stable for 30 days. For a study of patients with AIDS, we found that questions in this form did not fit the answers of respondents, because their symptoms (and ability to climb stairs) varied widely from day to day.

Example 2.14: On days when you drink any alcohol at all, how many drinks do you usually have?

Comment: Questions asking about "usual" behavior are common. However, they all impose the assumption of regularity on respondents. The question can accommodate some variability, but it is poorly suited to major variability. For example, if a respondent drinks much more on weekends than on weekdays, it is not clear at all how the question should be answered. Questions using the term "usual" need to be scrutinized closely to make sure the answers fit the reality to be described.

Example 2.15: How many miles are you from the nearest hospital?

Comment: It is easy to think that a respondent might know the exact location of the nearest hospital, yet have a poor notion of the number of miles. Moreover, although miles may be a good measure of distance in a rural or suburban area, time via the likely mode of transportation might be a more appropriate metric for a city dweller and provide the units in which respondents could answer most accurately.

Asking people questions to which they know the answers is important. However, it is easy to overlook the next essential step—giving respondent an answer task they can perform and that fits the true answer to the question.

REDUCING THE EFFECT OF
SOCIAL DESIRABILITY ON ANSWERS

Studies of response accuracy suggest the tendency for respondents to distort answers in ways that will make them look better or will avoid making them look bad. Locander, Sudman, and Bradburn (1976) found that convictions for drunken driving and experience with bankruptcy were reported very poorly in surveys. Clearly, such events are significant enough that they are unlikely to have been forgotten; the explanation for poor reporting must be that people are reluctant to report such events about themselves. However, the effects of social desirability are much more pervasive than such extreme examples.

For example, when Cannell, Fisher, and Bakker (1965) coded the reasons for hospitalization by the likelihood that the condition leading to the hospitalization might be embarrassing or life-threatening, they found that the hospitalizations associated with the most threatening conditions were significantly less likely to be reported in a health survey. Record-check studies of health conditions, comparing survey reports with medical records, suggest that conditions that might be thought to be embarrassing or life threatening were less well reported in survey interviews (Cannell, Marquis, & Laurent 1977; Cannell & Fowler, 1965; Madow, 1967). Distortion can also produce overreporting. Anderson, Silver, and Abramson (1988) found notable overreporting of voting in elections.

Although social desirability has been used as a blanket term for these phenomena, there are probably several different forces operating to produce the response effects described above. First, there is no doubt some tendency for respondents to want to make themselves look good and to avoid looking bad. In addition, sometimes surveys ask questions the answers to which could actually pose a threat to respondents. When surveys ask about illegal drug use, about drinking alcohol to excess, or about the number of sexual partners that people have had, the answers, if revealed, could expose respondents to divorce proceedings, loss of jobs, or even criminal prosecution. When the answer to a survey question poses such a risk for respondents, it is easy to understand why some respondents might prefer to distort the answer rather than to take a chance on giving an accurate answer, even if the risk of improper disclosure is deemed to be small.

Third, in a related but slightly different way, response distortion may come about because the literally accurate answer is not the way the respondent wants to think about him- or herself. When respondents distort answers about not drinking to excess or voting behavior, it may have as much to do with respondents managing their own self-images as managing the images that others have of them.

It is fundamental to understand that the problem is not "sensitive questions" but "sensitive answers." Questions tend to be categorized as "sensitive" if a "yes" answer is likely to be judged by society as undesirable behavior. However, for those for whom the answer is "no," questions about any particular behavior are not sensitive. When Sudman and Bradburn (1982) asked respondents to rate questions with respect to sensitivity, the question rated highest was how often people masturbated. Presumably its high rating stemmed from a combination of the facts that people felt that a positive answer was not consistent with the image they wanted to project and that it is a very prevalent behavior. Questions about drug use or drunk driving are not sensitive to people who do not use drugs or drive after drinking.

It also is important to remember that people vary in what they consider to be sensitive. For example, asking whether or not people have a library card apparently is a fairly sensitive question; some people interpret a "no" answer as indicating something negative about themselves (Parry & Crossley, 1950). Library card ownership is considerably overreported. Also recall that the event of going to a hospital, which normally is not a particularly sensitive question, can be a sensitive topic for respondents who are hospitalized for conditions that embarrass them or that they consider to be personal.

Thinking broadly about the reasons for distorting answers leads to the notion that the whole interview experience should be set up in a way to minimize the forces on respondents to distort answers. Some of the steps affect data collection procedures, rather than question design per se. The next part of this chapter will outline some of the data collection strategies that can help minimize those forces. This may seem a digression. However, the integration of data collection procedures and question design is critical to collecting good data about sensitive topics. The balance of this section will be devoted to question design strategies that can reduce distortion.

Data Collection Procedures

There are three general classes of steps a researcher can take to reduce response distortion:

1. assure confidentiality of responses and communicate effectively that protection is in place
2. communicate as clearly as possible the priority of response accuracy
3. reduce the role of an interviewer in the data collection process.

Confidentiality. Survey researchers routinely assure respondents that their answers will be confidential. Protecting confidentiality includes numerous steps such as:

1. minimizing the use of names or other easy identifiers
2. dissociating identifiers from survey responses
3. keeping survey forms in locked files
4. keeping nonstaff people away from completed survey answers
5. seeing to the proper disposal of survey instruments.

In addition, when survey researchers are collecting data that distinctively put people at risk, for example when they were asking about behaviors that violate laws, they can get legal protection from subpoena. Discussions of these issues is found in somewhat more detail in Fowler (1993) and in much greater detail in Sieber (1992).

The key threat to confidentiality is the ability to link an individual to the answers. One of the best ways to avoid that possibility is never to have information about which individual goes with which response. This can be done by using mail or self-administered procedures with no identifiers associated with returns. When there are identifiers, researchers can minimize risks by destroying the link between the respondents and their answers at the earliest possible moment.

However, it is only when respondents understand and believe that they are protected that such steps can result in reduced distortion of survey responses. If there are limits to the extent to which people are protected, ethical research requires that those limits be communicated to respondents as well. If researchers think that the limits to confidentiality they can promise would reasonably affect answers, they should change the procedures to create a condition that is more conducive to accurate reporting.

Emphasizing the Importance of Accuracy. Sometimes, the goals of a survey interview are not clear. In particular, when there is an interviewer involved, there are rules that govern interactions between people that may interfere with the goal of getting accurate reports. Routinely, when we relate to people, we like to put a positive sheen on the way we present ourselves; we like to accentuate the positive; we like to please the other person; we like to minimize stressful topics. Forces such as these may undermine the accuracy of survey answers. To the extent that respondents are following such guidelines, rather than trying to answer as accurately as possible, they are likely to give distorted answers.

There are several steps that researchers can take to reduce the forces to distort interviews. One of the simplest is to have interviewers explicitly explain to respondents that giving accurate answers is the most important thing they can do (Cannell, Groves, Magilavy, Mathiowetz, & Miller, 1987; Cannell, Oksenberg, & Converse, 1977).

Routine interviewer training urges interviewers to minimize the personal side of their relationships with respondents. They are not to tell stories about themselves. They are not to express personal opinions. They are supposed to say there are no right or wrong answers. They are supposed to establish as professional a relationship as is feasible (see Fowler & Mangione, 1990).

In addition, Cannell has demonstrated that interviewer behavior can be systematically manipulated to improve reporting in ways that are probably relevant to response distortion as well. Three specific strategies that have been evaluated by Cannell and his associates (Cannell, Oksenberg, & Converse, 1977; Cannell et al., 1987):

1. Interviewers read a specific instruction emphasizing to respondents that providing accurate answers is what the interview is about and is the priority of the interview.
2. Respondents are asked to verbally or in writing make a commitment to give accurate answers during the interview.
3. Interviewers are trained to reinforce thoughtful answers, and not to reinforce behaviors that are inconsistent with giving complete and accurate answers.

Some of these behaviors are designed to encourage working for complete and accurate recall. They also serve the function of asserting the primacy of accuracy over other goals. Cannell, Miller, and Oksenberg

(1981) found that these procedures, for example, seem to reduce the number of books well-educated people reported reading during the past year, which they interpret as reducing social desirability bias in answers.

Reducing the Role of Interviewer. How interviewers affect reporting potentially sensitive information has been a matter of some debate. On the one hand, interviewers can help to motivate respondents, reassure them that they are protected, establish rapport, and thereby increase the likelihood that respondents will answer questions accurately. Alternatively, the fact of presenting oneself to another person through one's answers increases the forces to distort answers in a positive way. The data on this topic do not always support one view or the other; there probably is truth in both. Nonetheless, there is considerable evidence that having people answer questions in a self-administered form, rather than giving answers to an interviewer, may reduce the extent to which people distort answers in a socially desirable direction (Aquilino & Losciuto, 1990; Fowler, 1993; Mangione, Hingson, & Barret, 1982).

In addition to using procedures that do not involve an interviewer, such as a mail survey or a group-administered survey for which people fill out questionnaires and drop them in boxes, there are at least three ways that surveys using interviewers can be modified to reduce the effect of the interviewer on the data collection process.

First, a very well-developed strategy is to have a series of questions put in a self-administered form. The interviewer can hand a booklet of questions to the respondents, the respondents can fill out the questions without the interviewer seeing the answers, and they can put the answers in a sealed envelope. A recent study of drug use clearly demonstrated that the respondents were much more likely to report current or recent drug use in a self-administered form than in response to questions posed by an interviewer (Turner, Lessler, & Gfroerer, 1992).

Second, a modern variation on that is made possible with computer-assisted personal interviewing (CAPI). With such data collection procedures, questions appear on a screen and are answered by some data entry process. If there is a series of questions that the researcher wants to keep private, the computer can simply be given to respondents who can read questions on the screen and answer for themselves, without the interviewer participating. For studies of people who come to fixed locations, such as doctors' offices, schools, or work sites, computers can be set up and used in a similar way to collect data from respondents.

Third, an innovative technique has been introduced into the National Health Interview Survey for a study of teen health risk behavior. In order to ensure the confidentiality of answers, and protect the teens from interviewer participation, sensitive questions are put on a tape player (such as a Walkman) that can be heard only through earphones. Respondents listen to questions read on the tape, then record their answers on an answer sheet. No observer, interviewer, or parent knows what questions are being answered.

All aspects of the data collection should be designed to reduce the forces on people to distort their answers, particularly when a survey covers material particularly likely to be sensitive. However, these are not substitutes for good question design. The next section deals with ways of designing survey questions to reduce response distortion.

Question Design Options

There are four general strategies for designing questions to reduce response distortion:

1. Steps can be taken to increase the respondent's sense that a question is appropriate and necessary in order to achieve the research objectives.
2. Steps can be taken to reduce the extent to which respondents feel that answers will be used to put them in a negative light, or a light that is inappropriate or inaccurate.
3. The level of detail in which respondents are asked to answer can be adjusted to affect how respondents feel about giving information.
4. Respondents can be asked to perform a task by which their answer is given in a code that neither the researcher nor the interviewer can directly decipher.

The Appropriateness of Questions. Probably no single topic gives survey researchers more grief than asking about income. Interviewers frequently tell stories of respondents who willingly answer questions that seem quite personal, such as behaviors related to the risk of AIDS, only to object to answering a question about their family income.

In this society, certainly there is a sense that income is a private matter that is not to be generally shared. In addition, people's willingness to answer questions in surveys clearly is affected by the extent to which they can see a relationship between a particular question and the objectives of the research. When someone has agreed to participate in research related to health or to political opinions, it is not self-evident why researchers also need to know the respondents' incomes.

Of course, researchers would say that income is an indicator of the resources people have, as well as the kinds of problems they may be facing. Information about income is helpful in describing and interpreting the meaning of other answers. When the purpose of a question is not obvious, it is only reasonable to explain the purpose to respondents. Although some respondents will answer any question, without worrying about its purpose, providing respondents with sensible explanations about why questions are included can only be helpful in getting them to give accurate information.

A variation on the same theme is that some questions seem inappropriate to certain subsets of the population. An excellent example comes from a recent series of studies aimed at trying to identify the extent to which people are at risk of contracting AIDS. Researchers wanted to find out about risky sexual behavior. One approach is to ask people whether or not they use condoms when they have sex.

Yet, in fact, condom use is relevant only for people who have high-risk partners or partners whose risk status is unknown. The majority of adults in American society have been monogamous or have had no sexual partners for some time. When people are confident that their sexual partners are not HIV positive, asking for details about their sex lives seems (and arguably is) intrusive, and it provides information irrelevant to risk of AIDS. However, for that subset of the population that has multiple sexual partners, asking about use of condoms makes perfectly good sense.

When we did our first survey study of behaviors related to risk of contracting HIV, our pretest instrument included questions about condom use and other sexual practices that increase the risk of transmission that were asked of all respondents. Interviewers and respondents had a great deal of difficulty with those questions; for many who were not sexually active or were monogamous, the questions were offensive and their purpose was hard to understand.

The interview schedule was then changed, so that respondents were first asked about the number of sexual partners they had had in the past year. In addition, respondents who were monogamous were asked whether their partners were in any way at risk. Once a group was identified that was either not monogamous or reported a high-risk partner, questions were asked about protection during sex. For that subgroup of the population, both interviewers and respondents could clearly see why the questions made sense, and the whole series went much more smoothly.

In one way, this is an example of thinking ahead about the purposes of the answers in a research analysis. Researchers should be asking people questions only when there is a clear role for the answers in addressing the research questions. In addition, the willingness of people to answer questions accurately will be increased to the extent that they can see the role that accurate answers play in addressing the research questions being addressed.

Managing the Meaning of Answers. One of the key forces that leads people to distort their answers is a concern that they will be mis-classified; that somehow the answers they give will be coded or judged in a way that they consider inappropriate. As a result, they will distort the answers in a way that they think will provide a more accurate picture.

Respondents look for clues to the way their answers will be interpreted. Researchers can reduce the distortion in answers by designing questions in such a way as to minimize respondents' perceptions about how their answers will be judged.

There are three general approaches:

1. The researcher can build in introductions or build a series of questions that minimize the sense that certain answers will be negatively valued.
2. The researcher can design a series of questions that enables the respondent to provide perspective on the meaning of answers.
3. The response task can be designed to structure the respondents' perceptions of how their answers will be judged.

One of the oldest techniques in question design is to provide questions with introductions that say both the answers, or all possible answers, are okay. For example, it was noted that people tend to overreport the extent to which they vote and the extent to which they own library cards (Parry & Crossley, 1950). One reason for this over-reporting is that respondents are concerned that researchers will infer that nonvoters are not good citizens or that people without library cards are not literate or have no literary interests. Some people who feel that such a classification is inappropriate will distort their answers, to make them more socially desirable and, indeed, perhaps to make them com-municate more accurately the kind of person they think they are.

Example 2.16: Did you vote in the presidential election last Novem-ber?

Example 2.16a: Sometimes we know that people are not able to vote, because they are not interested in the election, because they can't get off from work, because they have family pressures, or for many other reasons. Thinking about the presidential election last November, did you actually vote in that election or not?

Comment: The purpose of an introduction like this is to tell the respondent that there are various reasons why people do not vote, other than not being a good citizen. The hope is that respondents will feel more relaxed about giving a "no" response, knowing that the researcher knows some good reasons, some perfectly socially acceptable reasons, why someone might not vote.

Additional Comment: It should also be noted that both alternatives are presented in the question, with the perhaps rather feeble "or not." This particular question is not presented in a very balanced way. However, one clue that respondents sometimes use to investigator preferences is whether both options are given equal time, and thereby perhaps equal acceptability, when the question is framed.

Example 2.17: Do you own a library card?

Comment: When a question is phrased like this, there is a tendency for respondents to think that the researcher expects a "yes" answer. The negative option is not even presented. In fact, it turns out that people are more likely to say "yes" than "no" when asked this kind of question (which is a directive question) because both options are not presented.

Possible Alternative 2.17a: Many people get books from libraries. Others buy their books, subscribe to magazines, or get their reading material in some other way. Do you have a library card now, or not?

Comment: This question provides some legitimacy and some socially desirable reasons why the "no" response is acceptable. It tries to reassure the respondent that a "no" answer will not necessarily be interpreted as meaning the respondent is uninterested in reading.

There are studies of alternative question wordings that in some cases show little effect from these kinds of introductions. In other cases, they seem to make a difference (Sudman & Bradburn, 1982). When a researcher is concerned that one answer is more acceptable or socially valued than others, one step that may be helpful in reducing those forces is to include introductions to reassure respondents that both answers are considered by the researcher to be reasonable and neither answer will be interpreted as reflecting badly on the respondent.

Example 2.18: How many drinks did you have altogether yesterday?

Comment: Respondents tend not to like questions like this, standing by themselves, because of the possibility that their behavior yesterday was not what they consider to be typical. In particular, if yesterday was a day when the respondent had more to drink than average, he or she may be reluctant to give that answer, partly because it is seen as misleading.

Possible alternative:

Example 2.18a: On days when you have anything alcoholic to drink at all, how many drinks do you usually have?

Example 2.18b: Yesterday, would you say you had more to drink than average, less than average, or about the average amount to drink?

Example 2.18c: How many drinks did you have altogether yesterday?

With this series, the respondent has been allowed to tell the researcher what the usual pattern is and whether or not yesterday's behavior is representative and typical. Having provided that kind of context for the answer, it is easier for a respondent to give an accurate answer.

Loftus cites a similar example (Loftus, Smith, Klinger, & Fiedler, 1991).

Example 2.19a: Have you seen or talked with a doctor about your health in the last two weeks?

Example 2.19b: Have you seen or talked with a doctor about your health in the last month?

It turns out that different numbers of visits to doctors are reported, depending on the order in which these two questions are asked. When they are asked in the order indicated above, with the two-week question occurring first, there are more doctor visits reported in response to Question A. Moreover, Loftus has shown that the excess reporting from that order stems from overreporting. Apparently, when respondents have had a recent doctor visit, but not one within the last two weeks, there is a tendency to want to report it. In essence, they feel that accurate reporting really means that they are the kind of person who saw a doctor recently, if not exactly and precisely within the last two weeks. However, by reversing the order of the questions, those who have seen a doctor within the preceding four weeks are given a chance to communicate that they are the sorts of people who have seen a doctor recently. Then, it is easier for them to be literal about the meaning of the two-week question, and their reporting is more accurate.

No doubt, there is both a cognitive and a motivational component to why the question order has the effect that it does. Possibly another effect of changing the question order is to highlight that the researcher really means two weeks, rather than the more generic "recently," when the question says "two weeks." Nonetheless, the tendency to want to be properly classified no doubt is a factor as well.

There is a more general principle to be noted about the relationship between the length of the reporting period and social desirability. It is less threatening to admit one has "ever" used marijuana than to say one has done so recently. Conversely, it is less threatening to say one did not vote in the last election than to say one never voted. A key issue in both cases is what the answer may mean about the kind of person the respondent is. A reformed "sinner" (especially if the sin was long ago) and a virtuous person who occasionally "slips" are images most people are willing to project. A goal is to permit respondents to present themselves in a positive way at the same time they provide the information needed. Attention to the interaction between the reporting period and the message that answers convey is a part of accomplishing this.

Sudman and his associates cite another example of how allowing respondents to provide a context to their answers can improve the quality of reporting (Sudman & Bradburn, 1982). Once again, their focus is the quantity of alcohol consumption.

Example 2.20a: In general, would you say that you drink more than your friends, less than your friends, or about the same amount as your friends?

Example 2.20b: Think about the friend you know who drinks the most? About how many drinks would you say that person usually has?

Example 2.20c: And how about you? On days when you have any alcoholic beverages, about how many drinks do you usually have?

Sudman and Bradburn found that by asking the first two questions, the answer to the third question is, on average, significantly higher. The reason, they surmise, is that this series enables respondents to provide some context for their answers. Without questions such as A and B, the respondent is left to be concerned about how many drinks the researcher will think is "too many" drinks. There is pressure to be conservative, to downgrade the number of drinks reported, in order to reduce the chances of being judged negatively. However, given the first two questions, the respondent is able to provide some context about how much drinking "a lot" is in his or her social setting. The series almost guarantees that the respondent will be able to report at least one person who drinks more than he or she does. Given that anchor, it becomes much easier to report accurately on the respondent's usual behavior.

One other example from Sudman and Bradburn's research belongs here. Again, the question is about alcohol consumption.

Example 2.21: On days when you drink alcohol, how many drinks do you usually have—would you say one, two, or three or more?

Comment: In this question, the response categories themselves communicate something to some respondents about how their answers will be evaluated. Given these responses, one would be justified in concluding that three or more is a high category, the highest the researcher even cares about.

Alternative Example 2.21a: On days when you drink alcohol, how many drinks do you usually have—would you say one or two, three or four, five or six, or seven or more?

Comment: Readers will not be surprised to learn that many more people give an answer of "three or more" in response to this question than to the one that preceded it. In the first question, three drinks was an extreme response; in the second question, it is a much more moderate one. The response categories suggest the researcher thinks that some people drink seven or more drinks.

As a matter of fact, Sudman and Bradburn found that the very best way to ask this question is to have no categories at all; that is, to ask the question in an open-ended form and let people give the number. Although there are times when grouping responses may make the task easier and may be the right decision, researchers should be aware that the response categories provide information to respondents about what they think the range of answers is likely to be.

Finally, the perceived purpose of a question is affected by the subject matter of surrounding questions. For example, the meaning of questions about alcohol use may seem very different, depending on whether they follow questions about using cocaine and marijuana or questions about diet or steps people take to reduce their risk of heart attacks.

Example 2.22: Studies have shown that certain steps are associated with lower risks of heart attacks. We are interested in what people do that might affect their risks. For example, in the past 7 days, how many days have you:

a. Taken any aspirin?
b. Exercised for at least 20 minutes?
c. Had at least one glass of wine, can of beer, or drink that contained liquor?

Comment: Clearly that question will appear to be very different from the same question in a survey about drug use or drunk driving.

The common theme of the several techniques presented is to minimize the extent to which respondents feel their answers will be negatively judged. Letting respondents provide some evaluative context and minimizing the extent to which the researcher's judgments appear in the questions are both likely to help respondents feel freer to give accurate answers to direct factual questions.

Minimizing Detailed Answers

The above discussion included an example of when providing less structure to the response task seemed to have a beneficial effect on reporting. However, the opposite can be true as well. In some cases, it is less stressful to answer in broad categories than to give detailed answers.

Example 2.23a: To the nearest $1,000, what is your annual salary rate?

Example 2.23b: Is your annual salary rate less than $30,000, between $30,000 and $60,000, or over $60,000?

Comment: Most readers will no doubt feel that the second question will be less subject to response distortion than the first question. Of course, the answers to the second question yield much less information.

However, it is the lack of information, the lack of detail, which also makes the question more acceptable and less stressful.

In telephone surveys, a variation on this approach is used routinely. Respondents are asked about their incomes in broad categories, such as those in Example 2.23b. One or, sometimes, two follow-up questions then are asked that further break down the broad categories. For example, for those saying "less than $30,000," the follow-up might be:

Example 2.23c: Is it less than $10,000, between $10,000 and $20,000, or over $20,000? In this way, when respondents answer two three-response questions, they are actually being sorted into nine income categories.

Thinking about the level of detail in which answers need to be collected is an important part of the question design process. From an analysis point of view, it often is easier to collect information in greater detail, then combine answers at the analysis stage into bigger categories to yield useful data. However, that is putting the burden onto the respondent. In some cases, it may be best for the researcher to ask respondents to provide information in less detail. Such a strategy can pay off in higher rates of response and less response distortion.

Giving Answers in Code. In all of the above strategies, we have talked about ways of structuring the data collection task and the forms of the questions to increase the likelihood that respondents will give interviewers accurate answers. There is another class of strategies that absolutely prevents the researcher, the interviewer, or anyone else from knowing what the respondent's true answer is. Yet, the results can yield useful, analyzable data and estimates.

One example is currently being used in the National Health Interview Survey to estimate the rate at which respondents are at risk of contracting AIDS. The question reads like this:

Example 2.24: Is any of these statements true for you?

a. You have hemophilia and have received clotting function concentrates since 1977.
b. You are a native of Haiti or central East Africa who has entered the U.S. since 1977.

   c. You are a man who has had sex with another man at some time since 1977, even one time.
   d. You have taken illegal drugs by needle at any time since 1977.
   e. Since 1977, you have been the sex partner of any person who would answer "Yes" to any of the items above.
   f. You have had sex for money or drugs any time since 1977.

Comment: A "yes" answer does mean that a respondent has done at least one of the things on the list. However, it does not tell the interviewer or the researcher about any particular activity or risk factor. Only the respondent knows why he or she is at risk. Although it still may be socially undesirable to give a "yes" answer, it probably is easier to say "yes" to a question like that than it is to answer individual questions "yes" or "no."
   There is, however, a much more elaborate scheme that has been used to enable researchers to make estimates of the rates of behaviors or events that are highly socially undesirable or illegal. This method is called the random response method and involves the use of the unrelated question (Droitcur, Caspar, Hubbard, et al., 1991; Fox & Tracy, 1986; Greenberg, Abdel-Latif, & Simmons, 1969).

Example 2.25:

   a. Have you used marijuana in the last month?
   b. Is your mother's birthday in June?

Procedure: The respondent is given two questions, such as those above. Then a procedure is designed to designate which question the respondent is going to answer. The procedure must be one such that only the respondent, and not the interviewer, will know which question is going to be answered.
   Procedures that have been used include having the respondent flip a coin or having some system of colored balls that can be seen only by the respondent that designates which question is to be answered.
   Let us take flipping the coin, because that is the easiest one to explain. Suppose we have the respondent flip a coin so that only the respondent can see the result. We tell the respondent that if the coin comes up heads, he is to answer Question A; if the coin comes up tails, he is to answer Question B. The answer must be in the form of "yes" or "no."
   In this way, although the interviewer will know whether the answer is "yes" or "no," the interviewer will not know whether the respondent is answering Question A or Question B.

Table 2.1
Using Random Response to Make Estimates

	Response to All Questions	Estimated* Response to Unrelated Questions	Inferred Responses to Target Questions	Repercentagized Responses to Target Question
Yes	20%	4%	16%	32%
No	80%	46%	34%	68%
	100%	50%	50%	100%

*Unrelated question was whether or not your mother was born in June. One half of sample was asked this question. The other half was asked a target question, such as, "Have you used marijuana in the past month?"

How is this useful to researchers? Look at Table 2.1. Twenty percent of all respondents answered "yes." We know that half the respondents answered Question B, and the true rate for all those answering the question giving a "yes" answer is a little over 8% (i.e., one out of twelve). Hence, about 4 of the 20% yeses can be attributed to respondents whose mothers were born in June. That means the other 16% of the sample answered "yes" because they had used marijuana in the past month. Moreover, because only half the sample answered Question A, our estimate is that about 32% of this population used marijuana in the past month.

There are variations using the same idea that have been tried.

Example 2.26a: I want you to perform the following addition. Take the number of days in the past week in which you have used any marijuana at all and add to that the number of working television sets you have in your home now. What is that sum?

Example 2.26b: How many working television sets do you have in your home now?

Procedure: In some defined percentage of interviews, the interviewer asks Question A; in the rest, Question B is asked. From the sample asked Question B, the researcher is able to estimate the distribution of working television sets; hence, the difference between the mean answer to Question A and the mean answer to Question B constitutes the mean number of times the people answering Question A are reporting that they have used marijuana in the past week.

These techniques clearly have some drawbacks. First, they are time-consuming in an interview. Interviewers have to explain how they work to respondents and convince respondents that in fact no one can figure out what the answer means for a given individual. Second, to be credible, the choice of unrelated questions must be carefully thought out, so that people do not feel exposed either because the "yes" answer is such a rare event for the unrelated question or they think someone could guess what the answer is to the unrelated question. For example, in the second example regarding marijuana use, someone who smoked marijuana every day might be reluctant to perform that task because it would be unlikely that there would be seven working television sets in the home.

Third, the strategy for communicating which question is answered has to be one by which respondents feel confident that interviewers cannot easily guess which question they are answering.

An additional downside of these approaches is that individual level analyses are not possible. It also should be noted that the standard errors of these estimates are based on the number of people who answer the target question, not the number of people who are in the whole sample. Hence, standard sampling errors are larger when this technique is used than they would be if the same information were collected by direct questions asked of everyone. Nonetheless, it is possible to estimate rates for various definable subgroups from these techniques, as well as for populations as a whole.

These problems account for the fact that random response techniques, and their variations, are not very commonly used in survey research. In addition, perhaps because of their complexity, these techniques certainly do not eliminate reporting error. Nonetheless, on some occasions, they have been shown to produce estimates that look more accurate than what researchers have been able to generate from direct questions (Greenberg et al., 1969). Moreover, they absolutely do protect the respondents, because there is no way whatsoever to link a respondent specifically to a reported behavior.

Conclusion

Many strategies for reducing the forces to avoid socially undesirable answers have been discussed in this chapter. Some, such as the random response techniques, would be used only for a few key measurements that were thought to be extraordinarily sensitive. For example, if one wanted estimates of the rate at which people had done something illegal, and those estimates were central to the purposes of the research, it might be worth investing five or ten minutes of interviewing time to get two answers using random response. However, a well-designed self-administered strategy for data collection might be just as effective for improving the reporting of socially undesirable material.

For most research, the key messages are: ensure and communicate to respondents the confidentiality of answers; make clear to respondents that being accurate is more important than self-image or rapport with the interviewer; and design questions to minimize the likelihood that respondents will feel their answers will be put in negatively valued categories.

These steps are likely to improve the quality of reporting in every area of a survey, not just those deemed to be particularly sensitive. Researchers never know when a question may cause the respondent some embarrassment or unease. A survey instrument should be designed to minimize the extent to which such feelings will affect answers to any question that is asked.

CONCLUSION

There are many suggestions for designing good questions embedded in this chapter. The fundamental guidelines are to ask questions that respondents can understand and that they are able and willing to answer. To translate those principles into practice:

1. Avoid ambiguous words; define the key terms in questions.
2. Minimize the difficulty of the recall and reporting tasks given to respondents.
3. For objectives that pose special definitional or are recall challenges, use multiple questions.
4. Give respondents help with recall and placing events in time by encouraging the use of association and other memory aids.
5. Make sure the form of the answer to be given fits the reality to be described.
6. Design all aspects of the data collection to minimize the possibility that any respondent will feel his or her interests will be best served by giving an inaccurate answer to a question.

3

Questions to
Measure Subjective States

This chapter addresses the measurement of people's subjective states: their knowledge and perceptions, their feelings, and their judgments. As noted previously, a distinctive feature of the measurement of subjective states is that there are, in fact, no right or wrong answers to questions. "Rightness" implies the possibility of an objective standard against which to evaluate answers. Although the consistency of answers with other information can be assessed, there is no direct way to know about people's subjective states independent of what they tell us.

That statement does not mean that there are not standards for questions designed to measure subjective states. The standards are basically the same as for questions about factual things: questions should be understood consistently by all respondents so they are all answering the same question, and the response task, the way respondents are asked to answer the questions, should be one that respondents can do consistently and that provides meaningful information about what they have to say.

By far, the largest number of survey questions ask about respondent's perceptions or feelings about themselves or others. The basic task of most questions in this category is to place answers on a single, well-defined continuum. For descriptive questions, a dimension is defined such as hot to cold, slow to fast, or frequent to infrequent. Respondents are asked to place themselves, or what they are rating, on that dimension. If the question is about judgments or feelings, the rating dimension will be some variation of positive to negative. The majority of this chapter will be devoted to the design of such questions.

Questions designed to measure respondent agreement with or support of ideas raise some different issues, as do questions designed to measure knowledge. Separate sections describing those special issues are included at the end of the chapter.

DESCRIBING AND EVALUATING
PEOPLE, PLACES, AND THINGS

The following are some examples of question objectives. They are not intended to be well worded; they are intended to define the general informational goals that questions might be designed to achieve.

Example 3.1a: How friendly is your doctor?

Example 3.1b: Do you consider the president to be liberal, conservative, or somewhere in between?

Example 3.1c: How does the level of crime in this neighborhood compare with crime rates in other neighborhoods in the city?

Some questions in this category might seem to belong in Chapter 2, which concerned the reporting of objective events. For example, the answer to a question about crime rates could be thought of either as an objective measure of crime rates or as a measure of people's perceptions. Although people may agree on the friendliness of a particular physician, the liberalness of a president, or the level of crime, these properties are in the eyes of the beholders. If a respondent says a doctor is not friendly, the answer constitutes its own truth, even if others have a different opinion.

Questions about self perceptions are also covered here. Common examples include:

Example 3.2a: How frequently are you happy?

Example 3.2b: How interested are you in political events?

Example 3.2c: How likely are you to vote?

These are all questions that ask respondents to look at themselves, pull together information they have about themselves, and provide a summary of some sort. In addition to asking people to describe themselves, researchers also ask people to put those perceptions up against some standard, either an objective standard or a self-imposed standard.

Example 3.3: Would you say your current weight is too much, about right, or too little?

All of the objectives outlined above would be achieved by questions that have the same basic framework, which consists of three components.

1. What is to be rated
2. What dimension or continuum the rated object is to be placed on
3. The characteristics of the continuum that are offered to the respondent.

Defining What Is to Be Rated

Like all survey questions, when designing questions such as this, it is important that everyone be answering the same question.

Example 3.4: How would you rate your health—excellent, very good, good, fair, or poor?

This question probably has been asked in more health surveys than any other single question, and it has frequently proven to be a valid and useful measure of health status. Nonetheless, it may not be surprising to learn that the meaning of "health" is not consistent across all respondents. Some people key on the presence of health conditions, whereas others key on the extent to which they feel fit or the extent to which they lead healthy lives. Although these concepts may be interrelated, it is undesirable to have people answering different questions. To the extent that the meaning of health could be standardized across respondents, the question would have less variance attributable to interpretation of the question and, consequently, more true variance associated with the perceptions of the respondents answering the question.

Example 3.5: In general, do you think government officials care about your interests a lot, some, only a little, or not at all?

"Government officials" are a very heterogeneous lot, and which government officials a respondent has in mind may affect how the question is answered. For example, people consistently rate local governments as more responsive than state and federal governments. Elected officials may not be rated the same as those in the executive branches of government. To the extent that people's answers vary based on the way they interpret the question, a new source of error is introduced into answers, and the answers will be less good measures of what the researchers are trying to measure.

Example 3.6: Do you consider crime to be a big problem, some problem, or no problem at all?

Crime is also heterogeneous. Can people lump white collar crime, drug dealing, and armed robbery into a single integrated whole? It would not be surprising if respondents keyed on different aspects of crime. Moreover, this particular question does not specify a locus for the problem: the neighborhood, the city, the local region, or the nation. Which perspective people take will affect the answers. People generally rate the crime problems in their own neighborhoods as less severe than average. To the extent that what is being rated can be specified more clearly, so that respondents do not vary in their interpretation of what they are rating, measurement will be better.

The Response Task

Researchers have designed numerous strategies for evoking answers from respondents. The most common task is some variation of putting the object of the answer on a continuum. In addition, respondents may be asked to:

1. answer in an agree-disagree form
2. rank order several objects
3. answer in narrative or open-ended form
4. use magnitude estimation techniques

Each of these alternative response tasks will be discussed, starting with a straightforward rating task.

Defining the Rating Dimension. Figure 3.1 defines a continuum from positive to negative. Such a continuum can be described to people in numerous ways, and there are numerous ways people can be asked to assign answers to a position on that continuum.

Example 3.7a: Overall, how would rate your health—excellent, very good, good, fair, or poor?

Excellent	Very Good	Good	Fair	Poor

10	9	8	7	6	5	4	3	2	1	0
Best										Worst

	GOOD		NOT GOOD	

Figure 3.1. Some Examples of Evaluative Continua

Example 3.7b: Consider a scale from 0 to 10, where 10 represents the best your health can be, where 0 represents the worst your health can be, and the numbers in between represent health states in between. What number would you give your health today?

Example 3.7c: Overall, would you say you are in good health?

The above three questions are all using the same continuum. They are all asking the same question. They differ only in the ways in which the continuum is used.

In the first question, the health scale is divided into 5 categories, and each category is labeled with an adjective, from excellent to poor. The second question uses the same scale, but only the extremes of the scale are labeled; the respondents are allowed to use 11 different response categories, rather than 5; none of the middle categories is labeled with an adjective; and the respondents are free to use the numbers between 0 and 10 in any way they want. However, in both cases, there is a clear order among the response alternatives. "Very good" is better than "good" in the first question; eight is better than six in the second question.

The third question is a variation on the same theme. The continuum is divided into 2 categories, rather than 5 or 11. The positive category is labeled "good," and the negative category is labeled only implicitly as "not good."

These various differences among the questions have implications for resulting measurement. All of these questions define a single dimension, and they specify for all respondents a reasonably clear response task. Moreover, the fundamental assumption of ordinal measurement, that people putting themselves in a higher category on average are giving a more positive response than those who put themselves on a lower category, is very likely to be met.

Whether a continuum is labeled with adjectives or with numbers, there obviously is potential for people to use the scales differently. The level of health that one person considers to be "good" may be considered to be only "fair" by another person. To the extent that people differ in the way they use these scales, there will be error in the measurement. Anything that affects responses, other than the way that people see the things that they are rating, reduces response validity.

A critical criterion for a response task is that it define a single dimension, and that the categories of responses from which respondents choose have a clearly ordered component.

Example 3.8: How would you say you feel about your lawn? Would you say:

Very satisfied
Somewhat satisfied
Satisfied
Not satisfied

Comment: There are many observers who would say that "somewhat satisfied" is a lower, more negative category than satisfied. If some respondents concur in that judgment and use "satisfied" as the second most positive category, the ordinal assumption about responses would be broken, and it would create serious unreliability in the measurement process. If adjectival labels are to be used, it is critical that their order be unambiguous.

Example 3.9: Which category best describes your physician?

Very competent and businesslike
Very competent and friendly
Fairly competent and friendly
Fairly competent and not friendly

Comment: There obviously are two dimensions in the response categories: competence and friendliness. This particular set of response categories did not even play out all of the possibilities on the two dimensions in a systematic way. As a general rule, having respondents deal with two dimensions at a time is a mistake. Good survey design will ask respondents to place answers on a single, well-defined dimension.

Characteristics of Categories or Scales. When the goal is to have respondents place themselves or something else along a continuum, there are choices to be made about the characteristics of the scale or response task that is offered to respondents. Two key issues include:

1. How many categories to offer
2. Whether to use scales defined by numbers or by adjectives

In general, the goal of any rating task is to provide the researchers with as much information as possible about where respondents stand compared to others. Consider the continuum from positive to negative, such as portrayed in Figure 3.1, and the results of a question such as:

Example 3.10: In general, would you rate the job performance of the president as good or not so good?

Such a question divides respondents into two groups. That means that the information coming from this question is not very refined. Respondents who answer "good" are more positive than the people who said "not so good," but there is no information about the relative feelings of all the people who answer "good," even though there may be quite a bit of variation among them in the degree of positiveness they feel about the president's job.

There is another issue: the distribution of answers. In the above example, suppose most of the respondents answered the question in a particular way; for example, suppose 90% said the president was doing a "good" job. In that case, the value of the question is particularly minimal. The question gives us meaningful information for only about 10% of the population, the 10% who responded "not good." For the 90% of the population that answered "good," absolutely nothing was learned about where they stand compared with others who gave the same answer.

This analysis should suggest that there are two general principles for thinking about optimal categories for a response task. First, to the extent that valid information can be obtained, more categories are better than fewer categories. Second, generally speaking, an optimal set of categories along a continuum will maximize the extent to which people are distributed across the response categories.

Given these considerations, is there any limit to the number of categories that is useful? Is more categories always better? There are at least two limiting factors to the principle that using more categories produces better measurement. First, there appear to be real limits in the extent to which people can use scales to provide meaningful information. Although the optimal number of categories on a scale may vary, in part with the dimension and in part based on the distribution of people or items rated, most studies have shown that there is little new valid information provided by response tasks that provide more than 10 categories (Andrews, 1984). Beyond that, people seem not to be providing new information; the variation that is added seems to be mainly a reflection of the different ways the people use the scales. In fact, 5 to 7 categories is probably as many categories as most respondents can use meaningfully for most rating tasks.

A second issue has to do with the ease of administration. If survey instruments are being self-administered, where people read the questions to themselves, or are being administered in person, so that an interviewer can hand a respondent a list of the response categories, long lists of scale points do not pose any particular problem. However, when surveys are done on the telephone, it is necessary for respondents to retain all of the response options in order to answer the question. There clearly are limits to peoples' abilities to retain complex lists of categories.

When long, complex scales are presented by telephone, sometimes it is found that it produces biases simply because respondents cannot remember the categories well. For example, there is some tendency for respondents to remember the first or the last categories better than some of those in the middle (Schwartz & Hippler, 1991). When questions are to be used on the telephone, researchers often would prefer to use scales with only 3 or 4 response categories in order to ease the response task and ensure that respondents are aware of all the response alternatives when they answer questions.

A second independent issue is whether to use numerical or adjectival labels. The principal argument in favor of adjectival scales is that all of the points are more consistently calibrated by the use of words.

Consider the following question:

Example 3.11a: On a scale from 0 to 10, where 10 is as positive as you can be and 0 is as negative as you can be, how would you rate the movie you saw last night?

In such a response task, the two extremes probably are as well defined as they can be. However, there may be ambiguity about the meaning of "5." Is 5 a neutral point, where positive turns into negative? Does this mean that if someone's net feeling is more positive than negative, only scores of 6 or higher can be used? Alternatively, are people using the scale more like a thermometer or feeling ladder, really rating degrees of positiveness rather than going through a midpoint to a negative rating?

These are more than hypothetical questions.

Example 3.11b: Consider a scale from −5 to +5, where +5 is as positive as you can be and −5 is as negative as you can be. What number would you give to the movie you saw last night?

If 5 was consistently used as a neutral point in the first question, the one that went from 0 to 10, the results of these two questions should be identical. In fact, they are not identical. On average, people are more likely to report positive ratings using the second question than they are to report ratings of 6 or higher in response to the first question. Moreover, the distributions are not the same (Schwarz, Knauper, Hippler, Noelle-Neumann, & Clark, 1991). Almost certainly, people are inconsistent in the way that they use middle parts of the 10-point scale.

There is the potential to improve consistency by defining what meaning people should assign to the middle numbers. However, that sort of approach moves toward adjectival labeling of points. Probably, one can achieve more consistent use of scales by providing adjectives for all the response alternatives along a continuum.

The other side of the story is that it is difficult to think up adjectives for more than 5 or 6 points along most continua. When researchers have tried, some of the adjectival descriptions sound very close or similar to one another. It is virtually impossible to find a list of adjectives that will define a 10-point scale.

A related advantage of numbers is that a numerical 10-point scale is easy to remember and use. Thus, when doing telephone interviews, although it may be difficult to teach respondents 5 or 6 adjectives that they can reliably remember and use, it is comparatively easy to define a 10-point scale numerically. Hence, using scales defined by numbers can increase the reliability of a rating task performed on the telephone, if numerous response alternatives are to be provided. Moreover, it may increase the comparability of measurement of subjective ratings across modes of data collection.

Finally, a problem in international research and increasingly in re-search in the United States is how to get consistent measurement of subjective states for different cultural groups. In particular, when scales are defined adjectivally, it has been found that it is virtually impossible to have exact translations across languages. Adjectival scaling tasks across languages are not comparable.

It has not been well demonstrated that those problems are less severe if numerical scales are used. However, it certainly should be the case that such scales would translate better and more easily, because all that really is needed is a good translation of the two ends of the continuum.

In conclusion, asking people to answer rating questions using 2 or 3 categories constitutes an easier task for respondents and interviewers, but it provides less information per question. Using more categories, from 5 to 10, will provide more valid information about where people stand than rating tasks using fewer categories; more than 10 response categories probably adds very little valid information for most response tasks.

Finally, there are various occasions when using adjectival scales probably results in more consistent and therefore valid measurement. However, numerical response scales, with only the ends of the contin-uum defined, perhaps with some general discussion of how to use the points between the extremes, have numerous advantages and constitute a very good way to have people perform some rating tasks.

Using an Agree-Disagree Format

In the preceding sections, we have discussed asking respondents to classify or rate something by putting it on a continuum, often choosing an adjective or number to place it on the scale. The same kind of tasks can be attacked using an agree-disagree format:

The goal of such questions is basically the same as those discussed in the preceding section: to order people along some continuum.

Example 3.12a: I like Ike.

Example 3.12b: My health is excellent.

Consider the continuum from positive to negative that we have seen before. Both of these statements can be reliably located at the positive end of a continuum, either feelings about former president Eisenhower or the rating of a person's health.

Always	Usually	Often	Sometimes	Seldom	Never

Figure 3.2. Frequency Scale

Suppose a person is asked to agree or disagree with these statements. In essence, respondents are saying that their views lie at the generally positive end of the continuum within a reasonable distance of where they see the statements "I like Ike" or "My health is excellent" to be located.

Example 3.13a: I am sometimes depressed.

Such a statement would be located in the middle of the continuum indicated in Figure 3.2. It is somewhere between the statement that "I am often depressed" and the statement that "I am seldom or never depressed." If a respondent is asked to agree or disagree with such a statement, there is an interpretation problem when a person disagrees. A person could disagree because "I am sometimes depressed" seems to understate the problem or because it seems to overstate the problem. As measurement, the results are unacceptable. To be able to interpret the answers, a different point on the scale must be chosen for the stem question:

Example 3.13b: I am usually depressed.

Example 3.13c: I am seldom depressed.

Using the agree-disagree or true-false strategy to put rated objects on scales has several drawbacks.

1. The items have to be unambiguously at an end of a continuum, so "disagree" answers can be interpreted unambiguously.
2. The questions are often cognitively complex; disagreeing that one is seldom depressed is a complicated way of saying one is often depressed.
3. Even when four categories are offered (such as strongly agree, agree, disagree, and strongly disagree), the answers usually are analyzed in two response categories: agree versus disagree. Hence, such questions do not yield much information.

4. There is a tendency among less-educated respondents toward acquiescence, which leads them to be particularly likely to answer in the "agree" direction. That tendency leads Converse and Presser (1986), among others, to urge avoidance of this question form.

For measuring respondents' feelings about ideas or policies, questions in this form are difficult to avoid. Such questions are discussed later in the chapter. However, if the goal is to have something rated or placed on a continuum, a more direct rating task will almost always accomplish the same thing better. We can ask people to agree or disagree with the statement, "my health is excellent." However, how much simpler, direct, and informative it is to ask: "How would you rate your health—excellent, very good, good, fair, or poor?"

Rank Ordering

There are occasions when researchers want respondents to compare objects on some dimension.

Example 3.14: Which candidate do you prefer?

Example 3.15: What do you consider to be the most important problem facing the city?

Example 3.16: Here are some factors some people consider when deciding where to live. Which is most important to you?

Proximity to work
Quality of schools
Parks
Safety
Access to shopping

Example 3.17: I'm going to read you a list of candidates. I want you to tell me which you consider to be the most liberal.

The basic question objectives can all be met in one of four ways:

Task 1. Respondents can be given a list of options and asked to rank order them from top to bottom on some continuum.

Task 2. Respondents can be given a list of options and asked to name the most (2nd most, 3rd most, etc.) extreme on the rating dimension.

Task 3. Respondents can be asked a series of paired comparisons, ordering two options at a time

Task 4. Respondents can be given a list and asked to rate each one using some scale (rather than just putting them in order or picking one or more of the most extreme).

If there is a short list of options, Task 1 is not hard to do. However, as the list becomes longer, the task is harder, soon becoming impossible on the telephone when respondents cannot see all the options.

Task 2 is easier than Task 1 when the list is long (or even when the list is short). Often researchers are satisfied to know which are the one or two most important, rather than having a complete rank ordering. In that case, Task 2 is attractive.

Psychometricians often like the paired comparison approach, by which each alternative is compared with every other, one pair at a time. However, it is such a time-consuming and cumbersome way to create an ordered list that it seldom is used in general surveys.

Best of all may be Task 4. The task is probably easiest of all for respondents, regardless of data collection mode. Moreover, the rank ordering tasks (Tasks 1 through 3) do not provide any information about where the items are located on the rating continuum. They could all be perceived as very high or very low, and the rank order provides no information.

Task 4 provides information about where the items are located on the rating scale. Although there can be ties, so ordering is not known perfectly, usually an aggregate order will result as well. For all these reasons, very often a series of ratings, rather than a rank order task, is the best way to achieve these objectives.

The Role of Open-Ended or Narrative Questions

When the goal is to place answers on a continuum, allowing people to answer in their own words will not do.

Consider a question such as:

Example 3.18: How is it going?

People can answer in all kinds of ways, Some will say "fine," some will say "great," some will say "not bad." If one were trying to order such comments, some ordinal properties would be clear. Those who say "terrible" would obviously be placed at a different point on a continuum from those who say "great." However, there is no way to order responses such as "not bad," "pretty good," "good enough," or "satisfactory."

A first step for questions in this form is to define the continuum along which respondents are supposed to answer the question and to structure the response task, the kinds of answers that are acceptable, so that everyone is working with the same scale and the same response alternatives.

The continuum must be specified, and respondents must be told how to use it, by choosing among adjectives or numbers. When respondents are asked how they feel about something and left to use their own words, invariably they will use words that cannot be put in an ordered format. If ordering responses is the goal, narrative responses cannot be used.

In contrast, when the purpose of a question is to identify priorities or preferences among various items, there is a genuine choice.

Example 3.19: What do you consider to be the most important problem facing your city government today?

Example 3.19a: The following is a list of some of the problems that are facing your local city government:

a. Crime
b. Tax rates
c. Schools
d. Trash collection

Which do you consider to be most important?

The open-ended approach has several advantages. It does not limit answers to those the researcher thought of, so there is opportunity to learn the unexpected. It also requires no visual aids, so it works on the telephone. On the other hand, the diversity of answers may make the results hard to analyze. The more focused the question and the clearer the kind of answer desired, the more analyzable the answers. Moreover, Schuman and Presser (1981) found that the answers are probably more reliable and valid when a list is provided than when the question is asked in open form. If the list of possible answers is not known or is very long, the open form may be the right approach. Moreover, although computer-assisted interviewing creates great pressure to use only fixed-response questions, respondents like to answer some questions in their own words. Although the measurement result may not be as easy to work with, asking some questions to be answered in narrative form may be justified for that reason alone. However, if good measurement is the goal and the alternatives can be specified, providing respondents with a list and having them choose is usually best. Appendix C presents further discussion of the use of open-ended questions.

Magnitude Estimation

The tasks discussed so far involved people using ordered categories or scales to rate their own subjective states or their perceptions of others. When defining response alternatives on scales, it is useful to use adjectives that can be differentiated and do not mean the same thing; however, for the measurement discussed so far, the distance between categories has not been assumed to have meaning. It has only been assumed that people in one category or scale point on a continuum are likely, on average, to differ from those who rated themselves either higher or lower.

Researchers would like to have people use ratings that provide more information than that. Even though it may be true that it is impossible to assign absolute meaning to a person's subjective state, researchers have explored the possibility of having people tell them something about the distance between categories or ratings beyond their ordinal position.

The technique that people have used that seems most successful at giving more absolute meanings to ratings is magnitude estimation. The following is an adaptation of how this approach was used to have people rate the social standing of people in different occupations (Rainwater, 1974).

Example 3.20: We are going to ask you to use numbers to describe the social standing of people doing different jobs. We are going to ask you to use the social standing of someone doing the work of a carpenter as a basis of comparison. Let us define the social standing of a person doing the work of a carpenter as 100. If you think the social standing of someone doing a different kind of job is twice as great as that of a carpenter, you would assign them a number of 200. If you thought the social standing of a person was half that of a person doing the work of a carpenter, you would assign them a number of 50. Using that approach, what number would you give to the social standing of a person doing the work of a high school teacher?

The purpose of this kind of exercise is to have people give numbers that have more absolute meaning and have some algebraic properties that most answers to questions about subjective states do not have. If we ask people to rate social standing on a scale from 1 to 10, those rated 6 would not be three times as good or high as those rated 2. People do not use that kind of scale in that way. However, the hope is that when given a magnitude estimation task, the ratings that people give do in fact have that kind of property. An interesting recent application of that strategy was to have physicians rate the difficulty and amount of work involved in various things that they do. The reason that the researchers wanted physicians to attempt to rate the difficulty of their work using magnitude estimation, rather than using a simple rating scale of the same thing, is that they wanted to relate the answers to another variable that does have absolute meaning: the amount of money physicians are paid for doing various services. The basic form of the questions asked was as follows: "If the work involved in performing an appendectomy is 100, what number would you assign the work involved in doing a cholecystectomy (gall bladder removal)?" In fact, the researchers studying the relative value of medical procedures and services mount compelling evidence that physicians were able to perform this task in a way that was consistent with providing real information about the relative value and difficulty of procedures compared with a standard (Hsiao et al., 1992).

Such an approach is not useful for measuring many of the subjective states that researchers want to measure. It takes a fair amount of training of respondents, which is time-consuming. Also, although the technique has been tried with cross-section samples, as was the case with Rainwater (1974), there clearly are advantages to having respondents, such as physicians, who are selected for their cognitive abilities (Schaeffer & Bradburn, 1989). As a result of all of these factors, magnitude estimation is not commonly used in surveys. Nonetheless, magnitude estimation is an example of how the measurement of subjective states can be stretched to provide more elaborate, and more analytically useful, information.

MEASURING RESPONSES TO IDEAS

The tasks discussed in the preceding section all were geared to having respondents place something on a rating scale or order items on a scale.

A large part of the survey research enterprise is focused on measuring people's responses to various ideas, analyses, or proposals. The content of such questions is as vast as the imagination of the survey research community. The common form of such questions is something like the following:

> *Example 3.21:* Do you favor or oppose the idea of sending U.S. bombers to attack Antarctica?

> *Example 3.22:* Higher taxes generally hurt the rich and benefit the poor. Do you agree or disagree?

> *Example 3.23:* In general, would you like to have more money spent on the parks and playgrounds in your neighborhood area or not?

An important distinction to be made in thinking about questions like these is the nature of the task confronting the respondent. In the first section, respondents were asked to place themselves or others on some defined continuum. For example, they would be asked to rate their own health on a scale from excellent to poor or they would be asked to rate the job they thought that the president of the United States was doing from good to poor. The task posed by these questions, however, is somewhat different. Instead of placing some object on a defined continuum, the respondents are asked to rate the distance between their own views or preferences and the idea expressed in the question.

Consider the question about respondents favoring or opposing a bombing mission. Presumably, the respondent has some general opinions about how to approach the problem at hand. A policy alternative is outlined in the question. The respondents' job is to figure out whether or not the policy alternative is close enough to their own views that they can say that it is a "favored" policy.

In a parallel example, consider the proposition about taxes and the way they affect the rich and the poor. Obviously, this is a generalization. There is great potential for people to have perceptions that are more moderate or constitute only degrees of the extremity of the proposition as stated. Nonetheless, the task they are asked to perform is to look at their own views, in all of their simplicity or complexity, compare them with the statement, and decide whether the distance between the statement and their own views is close enough for them to say that they "agree."

The key difference to note is that respondents are not directly placing an object on a rating scale; rather, they are evaluating the distance between their views and a statement. The standards for these questions are the same, though: Questions should be clear to all respondents and the response task should be one they are able to do.

Example 3.24a: Do you favor or oppose gun control laws?

Gun control laws can mean many things. They can cover a range of policies, including rules about who can buy guns, how long people have to wait to buy guns, and what kind of guns they can buy. A fundamental problem with questions such as this is that what respondents consider to be the meaning of "gun control laws" can differ from respondent to respondent.

To the extent that researchers can minimize differences in interpretation of what questions mean, they can increase the validity of measurement. The goal is to have differences in answers reflect differences in where people stand on the issues, rather than differences in their interpretations of the questions.

Example 3.24b: Do you favor or oppose laws that would prevent people convicted of violent crimes from purchasing a handgun or pistol?

Obviously that is only one kind of gun control law. However, a question that is explicit about the policy that people are being asked about, that minimizes differences in interpretation about what the question means, should produce more valid measurement of where people stand.

There are occasions when is it reasonable to let people define terms for themselves.

Example 3.25: Do you think help with personal or family problems should be covered by basic health insurance plans?

The term "personal or family problem" is not defined in this question. The rationale for asking this question this way is that it would be very difficult to define what constitutes a problem for a person. The nature of personal problems varies, and a situation that constitutes a problem for one person may not bother another person at all. In such cases, it may be best to let each respondent define what constitutes a problem. Nonetheless, from the point of view of interpreting the results, the researcher knows that there may be great heterogeneity in the objective situations that constitute the problems respondents are thinking about.

Consider another example:

Example 3.26: Driving a car is not a right, it's a privilege.

That may seem to be a reasonable statement to some. However, it is an example of a very common characteristic of questions posed in an agree-disagree format: It is two questions buried in a single question.

One question is: To what extent do you think that driving a car is a right?

The second question is: To what extent do you think driving a car is a privilege?

It may be that the answers to those two questions are negatively correlated; the less people think driving is a right, perhaps the more they think it is a privilege. However, putting the two issues together may make it hard to interpret what the answers mean. People might disagree because they think it is both a right and a privilege. Because there are two continua underlying this question, researchers cannot reliably place "disagrees" on either one of these continua.

It is very common to find multiple dimensions underlying questions posed in the agree-disagree format, or variations thereon. The following are examples, cited by Robinson and Shaver (1973), that have this characteristic:

Example 3.27: America is getting so far away from the true American way of life that force may be necessary to restore it.

Three issues: How far America is from the true American way, whether or not the true American way should be restored, and whether or not force may be needed (or desirable) to restore it.

Example 3.28: There is little use writing public officials because they often aren't really interested in the problems of the average man.

Two issues: Value of writing officials and how interested officials are in the problems of the average man.

Example 3.29: I feel completely secure in facing unknown new situations because my partner will never let me down.

Three issues: How secure one feels in new situations, the reliability of the partner, and whether or not the two are related.

Because there are at least two dimensions underlying these questions, when people answer the questions, the answers cannot be used reliably to order people.

Hence, there are two key generalizations about the kinds of questions that can be asked in this format. First, the words in the questions should be as well defined as possible to increase the consistency of respondent understanding of the ideas. Second, items should be carefully studied to make sure that only a single idea or question is being presented.

The Response Task

Probably the most common way to pose the agree-disagree task is the following:

Strongly agree
Agree
Disagree
Strongly disagree

Such a response task clearly violates the first rule of designing a response task for subjective questions: It contains two dimensions. The term "strongly" suggests an emotional component, a degree of conviction or caring about the answer over and above the cognitive task that is the central question. Better survey design would keep the response continuum cognitive.

There are two less frequently used approaches to the response task that avoid the emotional or affective component of the above scale and, therefore, are probably to be preferred.

Completely agree	Completely true
Generally agree	Mostly true
Generally disagree	Mostly untrue
Completely disagree	Completely untrue

Another response issue is whether or not to offer a middle category between agreeing and disagreeing and what it should include. There are two reasons why a person might not be able to agree or disagree. The position that would legitimately put someone in the middle of the continuum described above is the person who perceived his or her opinions to be exactly in balance. Somehow, the person agreed to some degree, disagreed to the same degree, and could not reach a conclusion about the tilt. When respondents are forced to choose, by not being given the middle option, most of them do so. However, offering a middle option often is popular with respondents and conceptually it makes reasonable measurement sense.

There is another group of respondents that sometimes chooses this residual category: those who do not know enough about the question or their own opinions to answer the questions.

Example 3.30: The United States should increase its foreign aid to Guatemala.

It is likely that some respondents asked that question would not have enough information about either the U.S. aid program to Guatemala or the aid needs of Guatemala to have an informed opinion about that topic. In such a situation, for someone to say that they have no opinion is not to say that their opinions are balanced between agreeing and disagreeing; such respondents are off the scale. When respondents are likely not to know enough about a topic to answer, they should not be put in the middle category of the scale. Some systematic strategy should be found to identify people who lack the information needed to answer the question. That topic will be discussed in somewhat more detail in a subsequent section.

Measurement Properties of These Questions

Questions in the agree-disagree format are relatively undiscriminating questions. Most analysts divide respondents into two categories, those who agree and those who disagree. The reason for doing this is that there is research that shows that response style may have more to do with people's willingness to choose the extreme response than with differences in the opinions being reported. The issue of the limited amount of information that comes out of a two-category response task applies clearly to questions like these.

Cognitive Complexity

It is easy to write questions in this form that are very difficult to answer. Particularly when researchers try to ask questions about the negative ends of a continuum, it often produces cognitive complexity.

Example 3.31: I am not satisfied with my work.

In the agree-disagree format, in order to say that they are satisfied with their work, respondents have to disagree with such negative statements. Disagreeing with a statement that says they are "not satisfied" is a complex way to say one is satisfied. In cognitive testing, it is very common to find that respondents are confused by the task of how to communicate what they have to say in this format.

Conclusion

The agree-disagree question form, and its variants, is one of the most used measurement strategies in survey research. When asking about ideas or policies, it is appropriate. However, although such questions seem easy to write, they require considerable care to produce good measures.

There are three main problems with these questions. First, many questions in this form do not produce interpretable answers, either because they are not on a clearly defined place on a continuum or they reflect more than one dimension. Those problems can be solved by careful question design. However, two other problems—that these questions usually sort people into only two groups and that they often are cognitively complex—are more generic to the question form. Although it is possible to design good questions in this form, it often is possible to design a more direct rating task that will accomplish the same thing better.

MEASURING KNOWLEDGE

In survey research, knowledge is measured in four ways:

1. Asking people to self-report what they know
2. True-false questions
3. Multiple choice questions
4. Open-ended short-answer questions

Example 3.32a: Are you at all familiar with the proposals to control gun ownership?

Example 3.32b: How much do you know about the new proposal to control gun ownership—a lot, some, a little, or nothing at all?

Obviously, the goal of the questions is the key to the choice of questions. Probably the most common goal of knowledge questions in general population surveys is to identify those who think they are familiar enough with a topic to answer questions about it. A related common goal is to analyze whether those who feel informed about a topic think or behave differently from those who feel less informed. For those purposes, self-described knowledge is a reasonable approach to measurement. In fact, some researchers accomplish similar goals with questions that do not even refer directly to knowledge:

Example 3.32c: Have you heard or read about proposals to control gun ownership?

Example 3.32d: Have you discussed gun control with anyone?

Both of these questions can serve as indicators of familiarity with an issue. However, none of the questions noted so far has the potential to evaluate the quality or accuracy of information that people have. Sometimes researchers want to measure what people know.

Two favorite approaches to measuring knowledge are to use multiple choice or true-false questions. True-false and multiple choice questions share three features as measures of knowledge:

1. They measure recognition, rather than recall;
2. They depend heavily on constructing plausible wrong answers; and
3. The number of right answers usually is an overestimate of the number of questions to which respondents know the answers.

Recognition is easier than recall from a cognitive perspective. We all have had the experience of feeling we would know a name or a word if we heard it, but somehow cannot conjure it up without help.

The importance of plausible wrong answers is critical to understanding what the measurement process is about.

Example 3.33a: Who was the 13th president of the United States: Millard Fillmore, Zachary Taylor, or John Tyler?

Example 3.33b: Who was the 13th president of the United States: Millard Fillmore, Thomas Jefferson, or Richard Nixon?

The question and right answers are the same, but most people would find the second question easier than the first because of the wrong options. Many more people would probably be able to rule out the wrong options to the second question than to the first.

Of course, neither question is as demanding as the open-ended form of the same question:

Example 3.33c: Who was the 13th president of the United States?

Example 3.33d: Which president was Millard Fillmore?

The strength of the open questions is that there are virtually no false positives; respondents either give the right answer or they do not. In contrast, in the multiple choice or true-false format, a random guess will pick the right answer at some rate. Thus, if 60% of the people answer a true-false question correctly, one might conclude that only 20% of the people actually gave the right answer because they knew it; the other 40% (equal to the wrong answers) could have given the right answer by chance.

The disadvantage of the open form of the question is that it may provide a low estimate of active knowledge, because some people who could recognize the correct answer, or retrieve it given more time, will fail to retrieve it in a survey situation. Moreover, the level of specificity required affects the results. There are many people who could correctly identify Fillmore as a 19th century president and who would get no credit in response to 3.33c or 3.33d.

Finally, three general points that apply to all survey questions apply particularly to measures of knowledge. First, for the short-answer question form, it is particularly important that what constitutes an adequate answer is clearly specified by the question. To the extent that deciphering what kind of answer is wanted affects the correctness of answers, the question will be a less valid measure of knowledge. Second, measures of knowledge are question-specific, just like measures of other subjective states. The same level of knowledge may produce different results depending on the question. Third, the value of a measure of knowledge is usually dependent on how well answers are distributed. If most people are in the same category (right or wrong), a question doesn't give the researcher much information.

MULTI-ITEM MEASURES

One of the important ways to improve the measurement of subjective states is to combine the answers from more than one question into an index (DeVellis, 1991; Nunnally, 1978). There are at least two reasons why multi-item indices can produce better measurement than a single item:

1. They can produce detailed measurement across a larger spectrum of a continuum than a single question (or do it with less burden on respondents).
2. By diluting item-specific effects, they can produce a better measure of what a set of items has in common.

Improving Discrimination

One of the earliest forms of multi-item measures was the so-called Guttman Scale. The following is an example:

1. Can you walk across a small room?
2. Can you walk up stairs?
3. Can you walk a city block?
4. Can you walk half a mile?
5. Can you run half a mile without stopping?

If the above questions form a perfect Guttman Scale, without exception, the number of "yes" answers would tell a researcher which of the things on the list a respondent could or could not do. If these items scale, everyone who can run half a mile can do all of the preceding things; if a person can climb a flight of stairs but not walk a city block, the person should also be able to walk across a small room, if the scale is perfect.

Obviously, the basic concept is that there is a dimension of a physical ability. Ideally, each of these questions defines a point along that continuum. By asking a set of "yes or no" questions, then looking at the answers as a group, one can figure out where along the continuum the person falls.

A slightly different application of the same principle can be used that does not assume the kind of order among items that the Guttman approach assumes. Suppose a health condition can affect people in various ways that may not necessarily be related. For example, arthritis could make it difficult to:

1. walk up the stairs
2. use a pencil
3. bend or stoop
4. reach high shelves.

There is no necessary order among these various ways that arthritis might affect function; problems with using a pencil are likely to be unrelated to problems with bending or stooping. However, it might make sense to ask questions about the variety of ways that function might be affected by arthritis, then combine the answers in some way to create a symptom severity index.

There are issues about how to combine items like this, particularly when they are not necessarily correlated and are reflecting different aspects or manifestations of the underlying condition. Should these all be weighted equally, or are some symptoms more important than others? DeVellis (1991) presents a much more elaborate discussion of how to combine items and the value thereof; however, the basic point is that asking a series of questions, then combining them, sometimes is the best way to produce a measure of a complex state, such as a health condition.

Measuring a Common Underlying Variable

Any time one is using a question to measure some dimension, the answer is likely to reflect the dimension the researcher is trying to measure plus some other things. Suppose we were trying to create a measure of the way that a health condition affects people's lives. The following questions are asked:

1. To what extent does your condition limit the amount or kinds of work you can do at your job?
2. To what extent does your condition limit the amount or kinds of things you do for fun and recreation?
3. To what extent does your condition limit the amount and kind of work you do around the house?
4. To what extent does your condition limit your ability to get around and to go where you want to go?

The purpose of these questions is to get a measure of the severity of the effect of some health condition. However, the answer to each of these questions is likely to reflect both the severity of the symptoms from the condition and the particular style of the individual or the demands on the individual in the various domains asked about. For example, the effect of a health condition on a person's ability to work might depend importantly on the kind of work a person does (for example, how much physical effort is involved) as well as on the severity of the condition. In a parallel way, the effect on recreation might depend, in part, on the kinds of recreational activities a person prefers. The avid card player or television watcher might be less limited than the avid swimmer or hiker by the same condition.

The point is that the answer to each of these questions is likely to be affected both by what we are trying to measure (the severity of the condition) and by the particular role expectations or lifestyle of the respondent. However, the unrelated components of the answers are also likely not to be related across questions. Hence, just because a person has a job that requires physical effort does not mean that he or she has active tastes in recreation or in the kinds of things enjoyed around the house. By combining the answers to these questions, it is likely that an index can be built that is less affected by roles than any particular question and hence more purely a measure of condition severity.

To take another example, suppose our goal is to measure psychological distress. The most common forms of psychological distress of which people are aware are depression and anxiety. However, people have different words that they use to code or describe these states. For depression, people use "sad," "blue," and possibly "down in the dumps." For anxiety, people use "anxious," "worried," "nervous," "tense," "flustered," and so forth. For any particular person, with some set of experiences, some of these words may capture the way they experience their psychological distress better than others. By asking several different questions, using various of these words, it is likely that researchers can produce an index that captures psychological distress better than any single question, with whatever idiosyncrasies of interpretation or experience the particular words chosen bring with them.

When items are combined to produce a multi-item index, the index measures whatever it is that the items have in common. A multi-item scale is no guarantee that an index is measuring well what a researcher wants to measure. That has to be demonstrated in other ways. It does ensure, however, that whatever the items have in common is measured better than it would be with a single item alone (Cronbach, 1951).

THE RELATIVITY OF ANSWERS
ABOUT SUBJECTIVE STATES

The answers to questions about subjective states are always relative; they are never absolute. The kinds of statements that are justified, based on answers to these kinds of questions, are comparative. It is appropriate to say that Group A reports more positive feelings than Group B. It is appropriate to say that the population reports more positive feelings now than it did a year ago. It is not appropriate (at least not without some careful caveats) to say that people gave the president a positive rating, that they are satisfied with their schools, or that by and large they think their health is good.

In Chapter 2, the discussion of questions about objective facts noted that there are standards for right and wrong answers. Although sometimes the questions and definitions were complex, what was meant by being the victim of a burglary could be defined, and the accuracy of reports could be checked against records. If events are defined clearly, definitions are communicated in a consistent way, and questions are asked that people are able and willing to answer, the answers have absolute meaning.

In contrast, when people use a rating scale to evaluate their fear of crime or their feelings about a political candidate, there is not the same kind of absolute meaning about what a "good" answer means. Furthermore, the proof is that the answers that result from surveys are critically affected by many of the details of the way the question is worded and asked. The properties of the stimulus question have a critical effect on the response. The meaning of a response can be interpreted only in the context of knowing what the stimulus was.

Question Wording

If the answers to subjective questions were to have absolute meaning, the answers to cognitively equivalent questions should be the same. Often that is true. For example, it has been shown that substituting "surgically end a pregnancy" for the term "abortion" does not change people's answers to opinion questions on that topic (Schuman & Presser, 1981). Apparently, those words mean the same thing to people. However, Rasinski (1989) showed that people were much more enthusiastic about increased spending on people with "low incomes" than increased spending on people on "welfare." Schuman and Presser (1981) found that nearly half the population would support "not allowing" Communists to speak in public, but only about 20 would "forbid" it. The "meaning" of questions obviously can go beyond the literal interpretation of the words.

There are numerous examples of how small changes in wording, which seem to be equivalent, produce very different results. That is one of the reasons that interviewers are taught to read questions exactly as worded. Questions that seem to be the same often are not the same from the point of view of being a stimulus to generate a response about a subjective state.

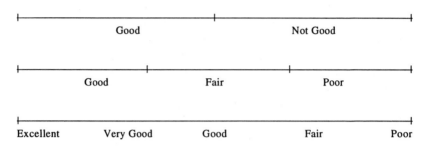

Figure 3.3. Three Scales

The Wording of Response Alternatives

The fact that the wording of response alternatives changes the distribution of responses is also clear evidence of the relativity of the measurement of subjective states.

Consider Figure 3.3, which defines an evaluative rating scale. On the top line, the scale is divided into two categories, "good" and "not good." On the second line, the scale is divided into three categories: good, fair, and poor. On the third line, the scale is broken into five categories: excellent, very good, good, fair, poor.

Someone might think that Scale 2 would simply divide the right-hand category, "not good," from the first scale into two parts. Similarly, one might think that Scale 3 would divide "good" from Scales 1 and 2 into three new parts. However, as some readers might already know, that is not how it works. People consider the whole scale when thinking about the meaning of categories. They consider the ordinal position of the category, as well as the meaning of the words. As a result, there will be many more people who rate their health as "good" or better in response to Scale 3 than do so in response to Scale 2. For that reason, stating that 70% of the population rates their health as "good" or better is an uninterpretable statement out of the context of the particular question that people were asked.

Order of Alternatives

The order in which response alternatives are presented to people also can have some bearing on how they answer questions. This is particularly true when respondents are given lists of response preferences that are not on an ordered scale. For example, consider a survey prior to an election primary. Respondents are read a list of several candidates, then asked which one they are most likely to vote for at the moment. Admittedly, an important characteristic of this particular survey task is that respondents may not be thoroughly familiar with all primary candidates. Nonetheless, it has been shown that when such surveys are done, the candidate whose name is read last disproportionately benefits and is disproportionately selected.

Even more subtly, it has been shown that the order of the basic rating scale, from excellent to poor, will affect the distribution of answers. When the alternatives are listed from poor to excellent rather than the other way around, respondents are more likely to use the negative end of the scale (Dillman & Tarnai, 1991).

Mode of Data Collection

For many purposes, it has been found that people answer questions in comparable ways by telephone, to a personal interviewer, or in a self-administered form (Fowler, 1993). However, there is some evidence that the way the question is presented, the mode of data collection, affects the way people use scales. For example, Bishop, Hippler, Schwartz, and Strack (1988) found that respondents answering self-administered questions used extreme response categories more often than those who were responding to an interviewer.

Context Effects

The location of a question in a survey instrument can also affect the way in which it is answered. Numerous studies have shown that the content of preceding questions can affect the way respondents interpret and answer individual questions (Groves, 1989; Schuman & Presser, 1981; T. W. Smith, 1991; Turner & Martin, 1984).

How "Don't Knows" Are Handled

A final important issue about the relativity of survey responses is the way that researchers handle the possibility that respondents are not familiar enough with the subject matter, or their own feelings on a topic, to answer a question. There are three different ways that researchers handle the possibility of lack of respondent familiarity with a topic. First, they may ask a screening question, explicitly asking respondents if they are familiar enough with a particular topic to answer a question about it. Second, researchers can include a "no opinion" option among the response alternatives provided to respondents. Third, the researchers can choose not to explicitly address the issue of respondents' familiarity with a topic; they can force respondents who do not feel they can answer a question to volunteer that information.

It is not surprising to find out that the results are quite different, depending on which of these options researchers choose. There is reluctance on the part of respondents to volunteer that they do not know enough about a topic to answer a question. As a result, many more respondents will choose that option if it is made explicit than will volunteer it. Moreover, in some cases, the distribution of answers obtained is different, depending on whether respondents are or are not explicitly offered the option of saying they do not have an opinion on a topic (Schuman & Presser, 1981).

Conclusion

It is important to differentiate between effects of question form on the distribution of answers and effects on the validity of the answers. For example, it was noted that when asking people to use the 5-point rating scale from excellent to poor, respondents were more likely to use the categories at the negative end of the scale if the negative end of the scale was presented first. This would change the mean or average rating to a lower level, but it might not change the validity or value of the question as a measure. The ratings emerging from the two question forms might correlate equally well with other measures with which they should correlate, which in turn means they are equally valid.

Another implication of this point is that the concept of "bias" in a measure of a subjective state essentially is meaningless. By changing wording, response order, or other things about data collection, it is possible to change the distribution of answers to a question in a positive or negative direction. However, the concept of bias implies systematic deviations from some true score. There is no true score in the measurement of subjective states, so the fact that a distribution is changed in one direction or another does not constitute bias. Moreover, if these ordinal measures are used properly, to compare distributions or parameters among groups from whom data were collected in a comparable way, the concept of bias in measurement is indeed irrelevant.

One of the most common abuses of survey measurement is people treating data collected using measures of subjective states, that are designed to produce ordinal measures, as if they had produced data with absolute meaning. When statements are made, such as that "most people favor gun control," "most people oppose abortion," or "most people support the president," the statements should be viewed askance. All that happened in any of these cases was that a majority of respondents picked response alternatives to a particular question that the researcher chose to interpret as favorable or positive. That same group of people could be presented with different stimuli that apparently addressed the same topic but would produce very different distributions and support very different statements.

CONCLUSION

In conclusion, there are four basic messages about how to design questions to measure subjective states.

1. Because there are no standards against which to evaluate the correctness or rightness of answers, standardization of the stimulus of the question is particularly critical in measuring subjective states. For this reason, designing questions that can be administered in a consistent way and that mean the same thing to all respondents, to the extent possible, is high on the list of strategies for creating good measurement of subjective states.
2. Equally important is standardizing the response task. That means clearly defining the dimension or continuum respondents are to use in their rating task and giving them a reasonable way to place themselves, or whatever else they are rating, on that continuum.
3. The distribution of answers that come from a question about a subjective state is relative; it has no absolute meaning. Hence, the mean or average answer to a question is irrelevant, indeed meaningless. Rather, the standard for questions about subjective states is the extent to which they provide valid information about the position of respondents in relation to other respondents. Generally speaking, the more categories respondents are asked to use, the better.
4. Combining the answers to several questions often is an effective way to increase the validity of measurement.

Having enunciated these various principles, in the next chapter we will discuss some specific strategies for designing survey instruments that provide good, useful measurement of subjective states and objective facts.

4

Some General Rules for
Designing Good Survey Instruments

In the preceding two chapters, we have discussed in some detail the problems associated with writing good survey questions and some general approaches to solving common problems. In this chapter, we attempt to lay out some general principles for how to write and design good survey instruments.

A good survey instrument must be custom made to address a specific set of research goals. It literally is impossible to identify the best question for a particular purpose out of context. Nonetheless, there are some general principles that affect the quality of measurement that emerges from survey questions.

WHAT TO ASK ABOUT

Principle 1: The strength of survey research is asking people about their firsthand experiences: what they have done, their current situations, their feelings and perceptions. Yet, surprisingly, a good bit of survey research is devoted to asking people questions to which most people do not have informed answers.

Principle 1a: Beware of asking about information that is acquired only secondhand.

For research regarding crime, people can report when and how they were victimized, when they feel safe and when they feel fearful, and what steps they have taken to reduce their fears or their risk of being victims. People can describe their experiences with calling the police, the response of the police to their calls, and the quality of their interactions with police officials. In contrast, most people cannot report accurately about the real rates of crimes in their neighborhoods or in their communities. They may have opinions about how well the police do their jobs, but, except for their own experiences, they are unlikely to have much specific information about police performance.

People are likely to have informed opinions about the schools that their own children attend. They are unlikely to have informed opinions about what goes on in other schools, in schools throughout their communities, or in schools throughout the nation.

Regarding their health, people can reliably report how they feel, what they can do, and how they see themselves to be affected by their physical condition. They may or may not be able to reliably report what their physicians named their health conditions or what procedures or diagnostic tests their physicians performed. People almost certainly are not the best sources of information about the medical name for their health conditions or how much money was spent to provide them with medical care.

To study the effect of race or ethnicity on employment opportunities, one can obtain descriptions of the jobs people have, their perceptions of the appropriateness of their pay or responsibilities, and whether or not they believe they have been treated unfairly or inappropriately by employers. Comparing the answers of people of different ethnic groups may be important to identifying the relationship between ethnicity and quality of employment. However, asking people for their opinions or perceptions of how fairly different groups are treated in employment situations is asking them questions about which most people are uninformed.

There may be occasions when it is important and valuable to measure peoples' relatively uninformed opinions. Such opinions and perceptions constitute a reality of sorts. If people think that crime is rising and the police are doing a poor job, those perceptions may be important in and of themselves, even if they are inaccurate by objective standards. However, researchers should not confuse opinions with objective results.

There are numerous examples of major differences between generalizations derived from people's secondhand perceptions and the results of their direct reports. Although the general perception in the United States is that the quality of schools has been deteriorating for years, most people report positive experiences with their own schools. Although in the early 1990s perceptions of ever-increasing rates of crime and drug use are common, in fact objective measures of rates of crime and drug use have been gradually and steadily declining over the past two decades. Although physicians report a perception of declining quality of life for people practicing medicine, the average ratings by physicians of their own quality of life are extraordinarily high. When studying a general problem, it often is tempting to ask respondents for their perceptions of the problems and possible solutions. Although the answers to such questions may be informative, in particular when they identify misperceptions or distortions, researchers should not forget the main strength of the survey research method. To repeat, the strength of surveys is to collect information about the firsthand knowledge and experiences of a probability sample of some population.

Principle 1b: Beware of hypothetical questions.

People are not good at predicting what they will do, or how they will feel, in a circumstance they have not yet encountered. Often researchers want to predict the future or estimate how people will respond to something new: a new television program, a new light bulb, or a new health care proposal. There are some reasons why this is very hard to do. First, behavior is largely determined by situations. Whether or not a person will give money to a specific charity depends more on how and by whom the request is presented than the particular cause. Questions about future behavior cannot reproduce the behaviorally relevant issues very well. Second, new programs or products consist of many components that are hard to describe fully in an interview. The researchers will pick out key features for a description, but it is hard to be sure the features that matter most to each respondent are included.

To the extent that questions about the future can build on relevant past experiences and direct knowledge, the answers will be more accurate. Women who have previously delivered babies do a better job of predicting their likely use of anaesthesia in a future delivery than women who have not had a baby. People can predict their buying intentions regarding products with which they are familiar better than if the product is merely described in a question; giving a respondent a chance to "try" the product improves the correspondence between reported intentions to buy and behavior. Nonetheless, in general, asking people to predict their response to a future or hypothetical situation should be done with considerable caution—particularly when respondents are likely to have limited direct experience on which to base their answers.

Principle 1c: Beware of asking about causality.

It is hard for social scientists to establish causal patterns. Many events have multiple origins. Few of us are able to report validly on the reasons we do what we do. Survey researchers often wish to identify the reasons for things, but asking the respondents to provide those reasons is unlikely to produce credible or useful data.

Example 4.1: Were you limited in your everyday activities because of your back problem?

Example 4.2: What is the main reason you did not vote?

Example 4.3: Were you homeless because of the high cost of housing?

Some people, whose only physical problem is lower back pain, may be able to answer Question 4.1, but people with various health problems will have difficulty sorting out the effects of back pain from those of their other problems to answer 4.1. Example 4.2 highlights the complexity of motivation and causality. Respondents can report barriers (trouble getting off work) or motivational issues (did not like either candidate). Yet, there will be people in exactly the same situations who voted anyway. Did we really learn anything interesting by asking people for the way they perceive causality—especially for not doing something? It is hard to make the case that we do.

Finally, Example 4.3 is the epitome of a question that will not produce useful information. Perhaps there are some people who would be homeless even if nice homes were free. For anyone who is interested in a home, however, their resources, their priorities, their standards for housing, and the cost of various housing features will interact in some complex way to determine if they do or do out choose to devote some of their resources to acquiring housing. This is known in advance, and it is hard to think what the respondents' analysis of these issues will add.

In general, surveys should address the things respondents can reliably report: what resources did they have, what were minimum housing requirements, and, perhaps, what is the perception of the cost of minimally adequate housing? The researcher can then describe the situation and identify conclusions that will be of much more validity and value than the respondents' analysis of causality.

Principle 1d: Beware of asking respondents about solutions to complex problems.

When decision makers are wrestling with options about how to solve problems, it may be tempting to ask survey respondents what they think.

However, if a problem is complex (and most of the hard ones are), it usually is necessary to have quite a bit of information in order to have a meaningful opinion about how to solve it. Surveys do not provide a good forum for providing much information to respondents, and response options necessarily are concise (which typically means oversimplified). Occasionally, an issue has received enough public attention that many respondents do have informed opinions about how to address a problem, but it is rare. It is easy for those involved in an issue to overestimate the level of information or caring most people have about their pet problem. Most often, survey researchers will be best served by asking respondents questions to which they have answers, leaving the design of effective solutions to problems to those whose job it is to address those problems.

Principle 2. Ask one question at a time.

Principle 2a. Avoid asking two questions at once.

Example 4.4: Would you like to be rich and famous?

Example 4.5: Are you physically able to do things like run or swim without difficulty?

Comment: Both of these questions are asking two questions, the answers to which can be different. Respondents could want to be rich but not famous; they could have difficulty running but not swimming. If a question includes two questions, and both questions are important, ask two questions, one at a time.

Principle 2b: Avoid questions that impose unwarranted assumptions.

Example 4.6: With the economy the way it is, do you think investing in the stock market is a good idea?

Comment: Sudman and Bradburn (1982) call this a one-and-a-half-barreled question (as contrasted with a double-barreled question). In the end, only a single question is asked, but the introductory clause asks the respondent to buy into an analysis of the economy. Admittedly, the clause does not exactly specify the state of the economy. However, the implication is negative. Moreover, the question imposes a relationship between "the economy" and investing that some people might not see.

Example 4.7: Do you agree or disagree: Given the amount of crime these days, it makes sense not to walk alone at night.

Comment: The question makes respondents assume there is a lot of crime and that the assumed crime rate should affect decisions about walking alone. If a respondent does not accept these assumptions, the question is very difficult. The question about how people feel about walking alone can be asked without the introductory assumptions.

Principle 2c: Beware of questions that include hidden contingencies.

A major weakness of some questions as measures is that the answers reflect what is to be measured only for a subset of the population. Such questions are limited in their analytic value, because they are not meaningful measures for the whole sample.

Objective: To measure fear on the streets.

Example 4.8: In the past month, have you crossed the street from one side to another in order to avoid going near someone you thought was frightening?

Comment: Crossing the street to avoid someone who appears frightening may be an indication of when someone is fearful. However, the relevance of this particular question has at least two contingencies. First, it depends on a person having been out on the streets walking. If a person is quite fearful, he or she may avoid walking altogether. A bit more subtly, fearful people may be particularly careful when and where they walk. Their patterns may be designed to avoid situations where they might encounter people of whom they would be fearful. To the extent that they are successful, they will have avoided those situations likely to produce the occasion when they would feel compelled to cross the street.

If everyone in the sample could be assumed to have had the same degree of exposure to walking on the street, then the rate at which they reported crossing the street might be an indication of either fearfulness or the extent to which their streets contained fear-provoking people. However, the question as written provides no such opportunity to sort out people's exposures. Moreover, even if it did, the fact that the rate of this behavior would be contingent on opportunities would mean that it would be an imperfect measure for classifying all people in a sample.

Overall, a more direct rating of how fearful people perceive themselves to be walking in the streets would almost certainly be a better approach to measuring fearfulness for all individuals in the sample in a way that would be analytically useful.

Objective: To measure social activity

Example 4.9: How often did you attend religious services or participate in church-related activities during the past month?

Comment: The obvious limitation of this question as a measure of social activity is that it is contingent upon church being one of the organizations in which a person is active. For all those people who are not affiliated with or interested in churches, the answer has no meaning as a measure of social activity. In combination with other items, there is a possibility this item could be a useful part of a social activity index. However the more generally applicable the item, the better it is as a measure of social activity.

Objective: To measure limitations on physical activity resulting from health problems

Example 4.10: In the past month, has your health limited your ability to do vigorous activities, such as jogging, swimming, or biking?

Comment: For those people who do these activities, the question may provide information about the extent to which health is affecting their lives. However, for the people who do not normally do such things, their "no" answer will mean something entirely different. Instead of saying that their health is not limiting them, they essentially are saying they are not limited because they do not normally do these sorts of things. This question can provide information only for that subset of the people who normally jog, swim, or bike.

WORDING QUESTIONS

Principle 3: A survey question should be worded so that every respondent is answering the same question.

Principle 3a: To the extent possible, the words in questions should be chosen so that all respondents understand their meaning, and all respondents have the same sense of what the meaning is.

Principle 3b: To the extent that words or terms must be used that have meanings that are likely not to be shared, definitions should be provided to all respondents.

Principle 3b is particularly important. Occasionally, one will see a survey for which interviewers will be given definitions to provide to respondents who ask for them.

Bad Example 4.11: In the past 12 months, how many times have you seen or talked with a medical doctor about your health? (IF ASKED: Include visits to psychiatrists, ophthalmologists, and any other professional with a medical degree.)

Obviously, such a procedure breaks the principle of having all respondents answer the same question and have the same stimulus. If some respondents are given definitions that others lack, respondents are answering different questions.

Principle 3c: The time period referred to by a question should be unambiguous. Questions about feelings or behaviors must refer to a period of time.

Example 4.12: How often do you feel tired during the day—always, usually, sometimes, rarely, or never?

Example 4.12a: Are you able to run half a mile without stopping?

Example 4.12b: How many drinks do you usually have on days when you drink any alcoholic beverages at all?

Comment: All of these questions assume the answers are stable over time and fail to specify a reference period. In fact, it is easy to think that the answers for a short time period (yesterday, last week) might be different from the average answers over a longer period (last month, last year). An acute illness, a holiday season, or a difficult period of work are examples of recent factors that could affect answers. If respondents choose to answer about different reference periods (one chooses the past week, another chooses the past year) their answers may differ for that reason alone. It is always good practice to specify the time period about which respondents are to report.

Principle 3d: If what is to be covered is too complex to be included in a single question, ask multiple questions.

Principle 4: If a survey is to be interviewer administered, wording of the questions must constitute a complete and adequate script such that, when interviewers read the question as worded, respondents will be fully prepared to answer the question.

Wording issues are somewhat different for questions that are self-administered, where respondents read the questions themselves, than when interviewers are going to read questions. In particular, when designing an interview schedule, it is important to appreciate the fact that an interaction is going on that potentially may influence the way questions are presented. It is important to design the questions to take that reality into account (see Suchman & Jordan, 1990).

Principle 4a: If definitions are to be given, they should be given before the question itself is asked.

Bad Example 4.13a: How many days in the past week have you done any exercise? When you consider exercise be sure to include walking, work around the house, or work on a job, if you think they constituted exercise.

Better Example 4.13b: The next question is going to ask you about how often you've engaged in exercise. We want you to include walking, anything you may do around the house, or work you do on a job if you think they constitute exercise. So using that definition, in the last week, on how many days did you do any exercise?

Experience shows that respondents are likely to interrupt the reading of a question once they think they have heard a question. When that happens, interviewers will vary in how conscientiously they read definitions, such as those in the bad example. By putting the definitions first in a question, researchers increase the likelihood that all respondents will hear the needed definitions before they answer the question, and they will make it easier for interviewers to read the questions exactly as worded.

Principle 4b: A question should end with the question itself. If there are response alternatives, they should constitute the final part of the question.

Bad Example 4.14a: Would you say that you are very likely, fairly likely, or not likely to move out of this house in the next year?

Bad Example 4.14b: If the election were held today, do you think you would be more likely to vote for Governor Clinton or President Bush, considering the way you see the issues now?

Comment: In both of the above examples, respondents are very unlikely to be prepared to answer the question as read. In the first instance, experience shows that respondents will forget the response task while they are concentrating on what the question is. In the same way, when there are dangling clauses at the end of questions, respondents are likely to find they can no longer remember the terms of the question.

Better Example 4.14a: In the coming year, how likely are you to move to another home? Would you say very likely, fairly likely, or not very likely?

This question puts the response alternatives at the end. The respondent can listen to the question, knows the response task is coming up, and then hears the terms in which the question is to be answered.

One final point about questions such as the one directly above: Respondents often will interrupt the interviewer before the response alternatives are read, if it is not clear that response alternatives are going to follow. In the example, a complete question has been read before the response alternatives come into play.

The reason for trying to avoid having respondents interrupt the interviewer, before the response alternatives are read, is that interviewers are then put in an awkward position, which they handle inconsistently. Suppose a respondent jumps into the above question, saying something like, "There is very little chance that we'll be moving in the next year." By the rules of standardized measurement, the interviewer should go back and read the whole question, including all the response alternatives. However, studies show that some interviewers will try to guess what a respondent would have chosen, had the standardized question been administered. It is in the interests of the researcher to try to provide a script that maximizes the chances the interviewer will present the question exactly the same to each respondent.

Probably Better Example 4.14b: Which of these categories best describes how likely you think you are to move in the next year: very likely, fairly likely, or not likely?

Comment: Including the concept that categories are coming up in the question probably will reduce the likelihood that the respondent will interrupt the interviewer before the whole question is read.

Another Bad Example 4.15a: Please tell me whether you consider each of the following to be a big problem, a small problem, or no problem at all.

a. Pain in your bones or joints
b. Difficulty breathing
c. Any other health problem

Comment: There are numerous problems with the example above. First, the question itself is not put in a form that constitutes a script for an interviewer. In fact, there is no question. It is almost certain that if an interviewer read the words above, the respondent would be unprepared to answer a question.

Better Example 4.15b: How much of a problem do you consider (READ EACH)—big problem, some problem, or no problem at all?

In that format, it is easy to see that there is a script for an interviewer. The interviewer can read the question as worded, filling in the various health problems from the list, and prepare the respondent to answer each question.
   Another common mistake is including "other health problem" in the question. Such a category is often seen in lists such as this, but in fact it does not constitute a viable question. In order to do anything at all with this question, the interviewer is forced to make up two different questions:

1. Is there any other health condition or problem that affects you?
2. Do you consider (ANSWER TO QUESTION A) to be a big problem, some problem, or no problem at all?

Even in this form, it does not make much sense. Moreover, as measurement, given the fact that only a few people will add "other problems" and there will be very little overlap among the "other problems," the analytic value of the results will be trivial. For most such series, not asking about "other problems" would probably serve the researchers best.

Principle 5: Clearly communicate to all respondents the kind of answer that constitutes an adequate answer to a question.

The easiest way to communicate to respondents what kind of answer to give is to provide a list of acceptable answers. Indeed, such "closed questions" constitute a major part of the survey research enterprise.

However, there are times when it is best to allow respondents to answer in their own words. In some cases, there are more response alternatives than reasonably could be provided, or the researcher may believe it is not possible to anticipate the range of possible answers. At such times, it is best to have respondents answer questions in their own words. (See also appendix C.) However, that does not mean the terms of the answer should not be clearly specified.

Example 4.16: When did you move to this community?

Possible Answers:

When I was sixteen.
Right after I was married.
In 1953.

Any of those answers constitutes an adequate answer to the question as phrased. However, they cannot be compared and analyzed. If some people answer in terms of how old they were, whereas others provide a year, there is no way to integrate the data into a single analysis.

The problem is that the question does not specify the terms in which the researcher wants the answer.

Possible Alternative Questions:

In what year did you move to this community?
How old were you when you moved to this community?

Either one of these questions communicates to all respondents the kind of answers that are acceptable and enables the researcher to easily analyze the resulting answers.

One temptation might be to ask interviewers to explain to respondents what is wanted, in the event that they do not discern it. Obviously that violates a basic principle that interviewers should be given an adequate script, and all respondents should be asked the same questions.

Another Bad Example 4.17a: Why did you go to the doctor the last time?

Possible Answers:

Because I wasn't feeling well.
Because my husband had been nagging me, and I decided it was time to go.
Because the doctor had scheduled me to come back.
To get a shot.

Once again, there is nothing in the question that specifies the kind of answer that is needed. Do we want to know what the medical condition or problem is that leads to the visit? Do we want to know what the impetus was (not feeling well, spouse was nagging) for deciding to go? Do we want to know what the patient thought or hoped was going to be done (checkups, shots, X-rays)?

The last three answers tell us nothing about the condition for which the patient was going to be treated. If we were interested in that, we should have asked:

Example 4.17b: For what kind of health condition or problem, if any, were you going to see the doctor?

We could infer that perhaps two of the answers (not feeling well, shot) were for diagnosis or treatment of a condition and not for a general checkup. The other two answers are ambiguous on that point. One approach to improving the question is to provide a list of possible answers from a single perspective.

Better Example 4.17c: Was your last visit to a doctor mainly because of a condition that you have had for some time, mainly to find out about a condition that you only recently noticed, or just for a general checkup, for no particular problem or condition?

Example 4.18: Where do you get most of your information about health?

Possible Answers:

From reading.
From newspapers.
From Ann Landers.
From the media.

In one sense, all these answers provide some information. The information is of a negative sort. The answers are *not* "from my doctor," or from "friends." However, the answers are very different. The question itself gives no clue as to how specific respondents' answers are supposed to be. When the respondent says "reading," does it matter whether the respondent is reading newspapers, magazines, or medical journals? When the respondent says, "from the media," does it matter whether it is from the television, from newspapers, or from the radio? In fact, the right answer for all the respondents giving the above answers might have been "Ann Landers." If Ann Landers was the principal source of information on health care, any one of those four answers would have been plausible, right answers.

The question itself provides no information to respondents about which level of detail is wanted. Moreover, there are no words in the question that an interviewer can use to stimulate the respondent to get to the right level of specificity. Some good, nondirective probing, such as "tell me more about that," will help to make the general answers more specific. However, to the extent that researchers can communicate to interviewers and respondents more clearly and consistently what kind of answer will meet their needs, they will have more comparable data from respondent to respondent, will make interviewing more consistent, and will have better measurement and data.

Principle 5a: Specify the number of responses to be given to questions for which more than one answer is possible.

Example 4.19: What was it about the brand you bought that made you buy it rather than some other brand?

Comment: Respondents will vary in the number of features they mention, and interviewers will vary in how much they probe for multiple responses. These sources of variability can be eliminated by asking:

Example 4.19a: What was the most important feature of the brand you bought that made you buy it rather than some other brand?

Comment: This form eliminates the variability in the number of answers given.

Example 4.20: Which of these forms of exercise have you done in the past 30 days?

a. Swimming
b. Jogging or running
c. Biking
d. Skiing
e. Working out on an indoor exercise equipment, such as a rower, Stair Master, or exercycle

Comment: The instruction (CHECK ALL THAT APPLY) is not consistently effective in a self-administered form; some respondents will check one box and move on. If an interviewer is involved and respondents are looking at the list of activities, this form may be all right. For self-administered forms and telephone interviews, however, a series of yes/no questions about each activity is a better question form. Interpreting a nonanswer to mean "no" is always risky and should be avoided.

FORMATTING SURVEY INSTRUMENTS

Principle 6: Design survey instruments to make the tasks of reading questions, following instructions, and recording answers as easy as possible for interviewers and respondents.

The job of the interviewer in a survey is intrinsically difficult. The main tasks are listening to answers, figuring out whether an adequate answer has been given and, if not, deciding what sort of follow-up probe to use to elicit an adequate answer. When designing a survey instrument, the researcher should try to make figuring out how to read the questions, which questions to read, and how to record the answers as simple as possible, so interviewers can focus on the real substance of the job.

For different reasons, it is important to make self-administered questionnaires easy. For the most part, respondents are not very motivated. In addition, it should be assumed that respondents are not facile readers. For both of those reasons, survey instruments should be designed to be as easy to go through as possible.

For an interviewer-administered instrument, some of principles enunciated above will be helpful. Providing interviewers with a good script, one that provides the needed definitions, and designing questions that communicate the kind of answers required will improve the ability of respondents to do their jobs and decrease the amount of work interviewers have to do. In addition, the simple mechanics of formatting the instrument properly can make the interviewer's job go more smoothly.

Figures 4.1 through 4.3 provide three examples of survey instruments. The questions are all the same, but the formats are somewhat different.

At least four conventions are basic to every interview schedule, and a researcher designing an interview schedule needs to attend to them in some way:

1. When question wording involves some kind of choice, such as when the interviewer has to decide on the exact words (he/she) is to read, a convention is needed. For example, when a question asks about a (SPOUSE), a convention such as placing the word in caps can be used to designate a place where an interviewer will choose between (husband/wife) as the exact word to use. All of the examples put optional wording in parentheses. Each has a slightly different, but internally consistent, way of presenting optional wording. All of these conventions serve the purpose of alerting the interviewer that a choice is to be made, and also maintain the principle of the researcher writing the script, so words can be read exactly.

2. A clear distinction should be made between instructions to interviewers and the words that interviewers should read as part of the question. SOMETIMES INSTRUCTIONS TO INTERVIEWERS

A1. On (REFERENCE DATE) were you working at a job for pay?

        1 [ ] YES (SKIP TO A2)
        2 [ ] NO

   A1a. Prior to (REFERENCE DATE), did you ever work at a job for pay?

        1 [ ] YES
        2 [ ] NO (SKIP TO A6)

A2. (On (REFERENCE DATE/ or your last job BEFORE REFERENCE DATE)
what kind of business or industry did you work in?

_____

A3. Were you self-employed or did you work for someone else?

        1 [ ] SELF
        2 [ ] OTHER

A4. What kind of work were you doing then?

_____

A5. Now, some questions about your current working situation. Are you currently
working at a job for pay, are you on *sick or disability leave from a job*, or are
you *not employed now*?

        1 [ ] CURRENTLY WORKING FOR PAY (GO TO A6)
        2 [ ] SICK OR DISABILITY LEAVE FROM A JOB (SKIP TO A9)
        3 [ ] NOT EMPLOYED (DO INTERVIEWER CHECK)

INTERVIEWER CHECK:

        1 [ ] IF R'S RESPONSE TO A1a IS "NO" AND R IS NOT EMPLOYED NOW
           (SKIP TO A20)
        2 [ ] IF R'S RESPONSE TO A1a *IS NOT* "NO" AND R IS NOT EMPLOYED NOW
           (SKIP TO A15)

Figure 4.1. Interviewer-Administered Interview, Version 1

ARE WRITTEN IN CAPITAL LETTERS, and the words that
interviewers are to read to respondents are put in lower case. A
different convention (Figure 4.2) is to place instructions to interviewers in shaded areas. The key is to have a consistent convention, so interviewers do not have to spend time and mental energy
during an interview deciding what to read to respondents and what
words are instructions to them.

  3. There should be a consistent convention to help interviewers deal
with skips in the interview schedule. Two of the attached examples
simply use written skip instructions keyed to particular responses.

A1. On (reference date) were you working at a job for pay?

YES
GO TO A2

NO

A1a. Prior to (reference date), did you ever work at a job for pay?

YES

NO ⊢—> GO TO A6, PAGE 2

A2. (On (reference date/ or your last job before reference date) what kind of business or industry did you work in?

A3. Were you self-employed or did you work for someone else?

SELF

OTHER

A4. What kind of work were you doing then?

A5. Now, some questions about your current working situation. Are you currently *working at a job for pay*, are you on *sick or disability leave from a job*, or are you *not employed now*?

CURRENTLY WORKING FOR PAY ‖ ——>GO TO A6, PAGE 2

SICK OR DISABILITY LEAVE FROM A JOB ‖ ——>GO TO A9, PAGE 4

NOT EMPLOYED ‖ ——>GO TO INTERVIEWER CHECKPOINT

5a. INTERVIEWER CHECKPOINT

1 IF R'S RESPONSE TO A1a IS "NO" AND R IS NOT EMPLOYED NOW
↓
GO TO A20, P. 5

2 IF R'S RESPONSE TO A1a *IS NOT* "NO" AND R IS NOT EMPLOYED NOW
↓
GO TO A15, P. 5

Figure 4.2. Interviewer-Administered Interview, Version 2

A1. On *(reference date)* were you working at a job for pay?

YES . . . . (SKIP TO A2) 1
NO . . . . (ASK A1a) 2

A1a. Prior to *(reference date)*, did you ever work at a job for pay?

YES 1
NO . . . (GO TO Q.A6, P.2) 2

A2. (On *(reference date/* or your last job *before reference date)* what kind of business or industry did you work in?

_____
(industry)

A3. Were you self-employed or did you work for someone else?

SELF 1
OTHER 2

A4. What kind of work were you doing then?

_____
(type of work)

A5. Now, some questions about your current working situation. Are you currently *working at a job for pay*, are you on *sick or disability leave from a job*, or are you *not employed now*?

CURRENTLY WORKING FOR PAY . . . . (GO TO A6, P.2) . . . 1
SICK OR DISABILITY LEAVE FROM A JOB . . . . . (GO TO A9, P.4) . . . 2
NOT EMPLOYED 3

IF R'S RESPONSE TO A1a IS "NO" AND R IS NOT EMPLOYED NOW,
        GO TO Q. A20, P. 5
IF R'S RESPONSE TO A1a *IS NOT* "NO" AND R IS NOT EMPLOYED NOW,
        GO TO Q. A15, P.5

Figure 4.3. Interviewer-Administered Interview, Version 3

The other example uses boxes and arrows to make it visually evident where to go. It probably does not matter which convention is used, but being consistent throughout the interview schedule, and being clear, will make the interviewer's job easier.

4. Conventions for recording answers should be consistent. Research organizations differ in how they ask interviewers to record answers. Some have interviewers circle numbers (version 3); some have them check boxes (version 1); some have them draw x's through the chosen answer. The particular approach is less important than that the survey instrument be consistent in having inter-

1. Since you last filled out a questionnaire have you:

   A. taken any medications prescribed by a doctor to relieve your prostate symptoms?

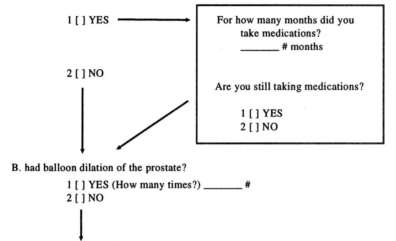

   B. had balloon dilation of the prostate?
      1 [ ] YES (How many times?) _____ #
      2 [ ] NO

2. How much do you worry about your health because of your prostate condition?
      1 [ ] A LOT
      2 [ ] SOME
      3 [ ] ONLY A LITTLE
      4 [ ] NOT AT ALL

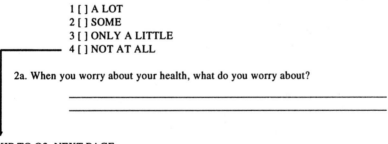

   2a. When you worry about your health, what do you worry about?

      _____

      _____

SKIP TO Q3, NEXT PAGE

Figure 4.4. Self-Administered Questionnaire, Version 1

viewers do the same thing throughout an interview, without having to think about it.

The two pages after that present some examples of self-administered survey instruments (Figures 4.4 and 4.5).

1. Make it obvious to respondents which questions they are to answer and which ones they are to skip. Most designers of self-administered questionnaires try to minimize skips. However, when they are

1. Since you last filled out a questionnaire have you:

    A. taken any medications prescribed by a doctor to relieve your prostate symptoms?

    YES ——>GO TO Aa   NO ——>GO TO B

    Aa. For how many months did you take medications? _____ # MONTHS
    Ab. Are you still taking medications?

    YES   NO

    EVERYONE ANSWERS:

    B. had balloon dilation of the prostate?

    YES ——>GO TO Bb   NO ——>GO TO 2, this page

    Bb. How many times? _____ #

    EVERYONE ANSWERS:

2. How much do you worry about your health because of your prostate condition?

    A LOT   SOME   ONLY A LITTLE   NOT AT ALL ——>GO TO Q3,
                                                        NEXT PAGE

    2a. When you worry about your health, what do you worry about?

    _____

    _____

Figure 4.5. Self-Administered Questionnaire, Version 2

necessary, maximizing the extent to which it is visually obvious to respondents, rather than relying on reading instructions, is probably a good idea. The two examples provide several approaches to making skips visually evident.

2. Make it as obvious as possible how to answer questions. Making the response task consistent throughout a questionnaire is probably helpful. Most designers of self-administered questionnaires try to minimize or avoid altogether questions that need to be answered in narrative form.

Probably the most important point, rather than any particular solution to these problems, is that issues of ease of administration be given priority in designing survey instruments. That may seem self-evident, but it is not uncommon to see survey instruments in which other things, such as saving paper or putting lots of questions on pages to make an instrument look short, are given priority instead. The priority should be on making instruments that are easy to read and easy to use for interviewers and respondents.

TRAINING RESPONDENTS

Any time a standard survey process is to be carried out, there is some orientation or training of respondents that has to occur. If the purpose of the question-and-answer process is to measure intelligence, ability, or knowledge, even then there will be some training and orientation of people taking the test: what are the priorities (to answer as many questions right as possible); what are the rules of the process (how long people can take; to what extent, if any, wrong answers are discounted); what are the purposes of each section or area of a test?

Principle 7: Measurement will be better to the extent that people answering questions are oriented to the task in a consistent way. It is undesirable that test scores reflect differences in understanding how to take the test (as compared with differences in the knowledge the test is designed to measure). In a survey, we try to minimize differences in answers attributable to differences in the ways that respondents are oriented to the task.

There are three areas in which respondents require training:

1. The priorities or goals of the task
2. The data collection process and how to play the respondent role
3. The purposes or goals of any particular subpart of the survey

It is in the interests of researchers to try to ensure consistent training of respondents in each of these areas. In Fowler and Mangione (1990), much more detail is provided about the rationale and importance of orienting respondents to their task.

When a survey is being done by mail, researchers must rely on written instructions. We know that respondents vary in how willing they are to read detailed instructions. An information sheet, such as that found in Figure 4.6, may be a reasonably effective way to get some of this information across to respondents in a consistent way. However, one of the prices of mail surveys is that there is less ability to engage in effective respondent training.

When an interviewer is used, the potential for effective respondent training is clearly enhanced. However, some interviewers are reluctant to assume that kind of orienting role when they are asking people to volunteer to be respondents.

Interviewers need to dissociate the issue of enlisting cooperation from the issue of how the respondent is to perform the job. Researchers can help interviewers by providing standardized orienting instructions for interviewers to use.

The following is an example of an introduction that Cannell, Groves, Magilavy, Mathiowetz, and Miller (1987) have used as a way of asserting the priority of providing accurate and complete answers.

> This research is authorized by the Public Health Service Act. It's important for the Public Health Service to get exact details on every question, even on those which may seem unimportant to you. This may take extra effort. Are you willing to think carefully about each question in order to give accurate information?

If the respondent agreed, the following statement was read:

> For our part, we will keep all information you give confidential. Of course, the interview is voluntary. Should we come to any question which you do not want to answer, just let me know and we'll move on to the next one.

We also know that respondents often do not know how a standardized interview is to proceed. As a result, interviewers find it extremely helpful to read something like the following before beginning a standardized interview (Fowler & Mangione, 1990):

> Since many people have never been in an interview exactly like this, let me read you a paragraph that tells a little bit about how it works. I am going to read you a set of questions exactly as they are worded so that every respondent in the survey is answering the same questions. You'll be asked to answer two kinds of questions. In some cases, you'll be asked to answer in your own words. For those questions, I will have to write

MEDICARE OUTCOME STUDY: INFORMATION SHEET

WHO IS DOING THE STUDY? The study is being done jointly by Dartmouth Medical School and the University of Massachusetts Center for Survey Research.

WHO IS SPONSORING THE STUDY? The Agency for Health Care Policy and Research, which is part of the United States Public Health Service.

WHAT IS THE PURPOSE OF THE STUDY? The purpose of the study is to get a picture of the effects of prostate radiation on a wide sample of men like yourself. It will help physicians and patients have better information about what to expect after radiation.

WHAT KINDS OF QUESTIONS WILL BE ASKED? Questions about your general health, how radiation affected you, and how you are feeling now.

HOW DID YOU GET MY NAME? Your name and address were selected from the records of the Health Care Financing Administration (HCFA), the administrators of the Medicare program. HCFA participates in important studies designed to help evaluate the effectiveness of medical care in different parts of the country.

DO I HAVE TO PARTICIPATE? Participation in the study is voluntary. In particular, you should know that participation will have no effect at all on your Medicare benefits. However, if you don't choose to participate, we will lose the benefit of your experiences and lower the accuracy of the study. If there are any questions you prefer not to answer, you can skip those questions.

HOW LONG WILL IT TAKE? The length depends somewhat on your answers. Some people have more to say than others. However, the average time to complete the questionnaire is about 20 minutes.

ARE MY ANSWERS CONFIDENTIAL? Yes. Your answers will never be used in any way that would identify you. They will be combined with answers from other respondents to make a statistical report. The ID number on the questionnaire and envelope are just so we know you returned a form.

HOW WILL THE DATA BE REPORTED? The research results will be reported in scientific journals and will provide important data for patient information materials that will be created to help patients who have prostate cancer decide how they want to be treated.

Figure 4.6. Example of a Fact Sheet

down your answers word for word. In other cases, you will be given a list of answers and asked to choose the one that fits best. If at any time during the interview you are not clear about what is wanted, be sure to ask me.

Such an instruction does two things to improve measurement. First, it teaches respondents what to expect. It makes them more likely to answer by choosing one of the categories provided or to answer slowly when they are required to provide narrative responses, so interviewers can record answers completely. Second, once interviewers have told respondents what interviewers do, it makes it easier for them to do what they are supposed to do and harder to behave in ways that are inconsistent with the way they are trained.

Finally, researchers often neglect efforts to provide respondents with an overview of the purposes of a series of questions.

Example: The next series of questions is designed to try to get a picture of all the different kinds of medical care that you have received in the last 12 months. We will be asking about doctors, going to hospitals, tests, and other things doctors may have done to diagnose or treat health conditions.

Having too many of these instructions may seem long and boring to interviewers and respondents. In particular, it is unlikely that respondents filling out self-administered forms want to read lengthy explanations for each section. On the other hand, such introductions can provide a sense of purpose and rationale to a series of questions, that otherwise might seem dispersed and redundant. More research is needed to know how to do these things best. However, almost certainly more use of orienting and explanatory introductions to sections of questions would improve the question-and-answer and measurement process.

CONCLUSION

The principles outlined in this chapter emerge largely from studies of the relationships between question characteristics and survey error. Many of the problems discussed can be identified by informed observation. Thus one approach to evaluating a survey instrument is to critically review a draft set of questions to identify those that clearly violate the principles outlined in this chapter (summarized in Figure 4.7). Some problems, such as whether or not a reference period is specified or whether questions include parenthetical clauses that should be read to everyone, can be unambiguously identified in this way. However, most of the principles enunciated pertain to how questions work for respondents and interviewers. To assess that, the opinions of members of the research team are no substitute for empirical testing. Procedures for evaluating questions prior to a survey are the topic of Chapter 5.

Principle 1:   The strength of survey research is asking people about their firsthand experiences: what they have done, their current situations, their feelings and perceptions.

    Principle 1a: Beware of asking about information that is only acquired *secondhand*.

    Principle 1b: Beware of hypothetical questions.

    Principle 1c: Beware of asking about causality.

    Principle 1d: Beware of asking respondents about solutions to complex problems.

Principle 2:   Ask one question at a time.

    Principle 2a: Avoid asking two questions at once.

    Principle 2b: Avoid questions that impose unwarranted assumptions.

    Principle 2c: Beware of questions that include hidden contingencies.

Principle 3:   A survey question should be worded so that every respondent is answering the same question.

    Principle 3a: To the extent possible, the words in questions should be chosen so that all respondents understand their meaning and all respondents have the same sense of what the meaning is.

    Principle 3b: To the extent that words or terms must be used that have meanings that are likely not to be shared, definitions should be provided to all respondents.

    Principle 3c: The time period referred to by a question should be unambiguous.

    Principle 3d: If what is to be covered is too complex to be included in a single question, ask multiple questions.

Principle 4:   If a survey is to be interviewer administered, wording of the questions must constitute a complete and adequate script such that, when interviewers read the question as worded, respondents will be fully prepared to answer the question.

    Principle 4a: If definitions are to be given, they should be given before the question itself is asked.

    Principle 4b: A question should end with the question itself. If there are response alternatives, they should constitute the final part of the question.

Principle 5:   Clearly communicate to all respondents the kind of answer that constitutes an adequate answer to a question.

    Principle 5a: Specify the number of responses to be given to questions for which more than one answer is possible.

Principle 6:   Design survey instruments to make the task of reading questions, following instructions, and recording answers as easy as possible for interviewers and respondents.

Principle 7:   Measurement will be better to the extent that people answering questions are oriented to the task in a consistent way.

Figure 4.7. Summary of Principles of Good Question Design

5

Presurvey Evaluation of Questions

In previous chapters, we have enunciated three clear standards for good survey questions:

1. What the question means and the kind of answer that will meet the question objectives must be consistently understood by all respondents.
2. Respondents must be able and willing to perform the tasks required to answer the questions.
3. Survey questions must constitute a protocol for an interaction, a question and answer process, that will be consistent across respondents, and, when they are involved, across interviewers.

In recent years there has been increased attention given to the evaluation of survey questions from the cognitive and interactional perspectives. The basic idea is that before a question is asked in a full-scale survey, testing should be done to find out if people can understand the questions, if they can perform the tasks that questions require, and if interviewers can and will read questions as worded. In this chapter, we discuss the alternatives available to researchers to try to find out how well their questions meet these standards before a survey is done. Although some form of field pretest is routine, using the full protocols discussed in this chapter would constitute a significant increase in question evaluation effort for most survey organizations. We hope to make the case that such effort is a wise investment.

There are three main kinds of question evaluation activities that are the focus of this chapter.

1. Focus group discussions
2. Intensive individual interviews (not replicating proposed survey procedures)
3. Field pretesting (replicating to a reasonable extent procedures to be used in a proposed survey)

FOCUS GROUP DISCUSSIONS

Focus groups have been a part of the social research arsenal of methods for a long time. Some common examples include:

1. Developers of commercial or political advertisements often pretest their products by having groups of people watch them, followed by a systematic discussion about what observers liked and did not like about the presentation.
2. Developers of new products and ideas present them to small groups, then have a discussion about what people like and do not like about them.
3. People running political campaigns bring small groups together as a way of trying to learn which topics people are concerned about and how they think about key political issues.

On one hand, focus groups seem so simple as an idea, it is hard to take them seriously. On the other hand, it is unusual for a researcher, no matter how seasoned in a particular area, to say that at least a few focus group discussions at the beginning of a study were not valuable. Systematic conversations with groups of people do not occur very often. Every researcher's perspective is limited to some extent. Listening to what people have to say invariably broadens a researcher's perspective about the realities to be studied or how people think about them.

In survey research, focus groups most often have been used to help define the topic and the research questions. However, focus groups also have a role to play in the question evaluation process. Using focus groups for the evaluation of proposed survey questions requires that there already be developed some clear ideas about what a proposed survey instrument would look like.

There are two main aspects of survey instrument design to which focus group discussions could contribute:

1. To help examine the assumptions about the reality about which people will be asked.
2. To evaluate assumptions about vocabulary, the way people understand terms or concepts that will be used in survey instruments.

Example: Researchers were planning a study of people's attendance at and participation in arts-related events and performances. A key part of the survey was to ask people how often they had attended certain kinds of performances. Several focus group discussions were conducted aimed at finding out what kinds of different arts-related activities people might think they should report and to examine specific wording of proposed questions.

With respect to what counts, one key issue turned out to be the problem of incidental arts. If a person goes to dinner and there is a jazz pianist at the restaurant, does that count as attending a jazz performance? What about music heard at fairs or amusement parks? There was little question in people's minds about what counted if they bought a ticket and sat down for a program of music. However, art and music are present in many places in society, and clearly people did not know what to do with incidental exposure to various art performances and exhibits.

In the course of the focus groups, researchers also became aware of some of the difficulties in classifying musical events. When asked for the frequency of seeing or attending classical music concerts, some respondents thought opera should count. Others wondered what to do when they attended or viewed programs that had a mixture of music, some classical and some not.

Even a term such as "watch a program on television" proved to be complicated. Again, intentionality was a concern. If someone else had turned on the program, and the respondent was incidentally exposed to the program, does that count as watching? Does one have to watch the whole program before it counts?

The above example is useful as an illustration of two different kinds of valuable information that can be derived from focus group discussions. First, focus group discussions can teach researchers about the complexity of the realities they will be asking respondents to describe. In this case, it became apparent that exposure to art takes place in many complex ways that the initial design of the survey instrument did not take into account. When researchers understood that people would have experiences that would be ambiguous, they could redesign questions to help respondents do their reporting in a consistent way.

Researchers also learned about ambiguities in the vocabulary they were using to ask questions. Terms such as "look at a program," "attend a classical music performance," or "go to an art exhibit" are not interpreted consistently. When people discussed phrases like this, it was clear they had different interpretations of what did or did not count.

Practical Procedures

Books have been devoted specifically to how to make focus groups useful and productive (Krueger, 1988; Morgan, 1988; Stewart & Shamdasani, 1990). The general principles for all group discussions, such as making people feel at ease, fostering communication, giving all people a chance to speak, and striking a reasonable balance between letting people express themselves and keeping the conversation focused, all apply to focus discussion groups aimed at survey instruments. Having a good leader, one with good interviewing skills, will make focus groups work better.

In our experience, groups of five to eight people are optimal. When groups are smaller, some of the advantages of diversity and energy from the group seem to be lost; the interaction feels more like three or four individual interviews than a group discussion.

When groups are larger than about seven, it becomes difficult for everyone to be heard. In particular, it may be hard for the leader to probe each person to find views and experiences that differ from the primary ones expressed. However, there are those who advocate groups of 10 or 12, particularly for topics on which some people may have little to say.

There is no way to generalize about the ideal composition of a group. It obviously depends on the topic. It should be kept in mind, however, that an important goal of the focus group process is to get a sense of the diversity of experience and perception, rather than to get a representative sample *per se*. The most important product of focus group discussions is to identify threats to standardization. Hence, one important consideration in constructing focus groups is to include people who represent a wide range of experiences and perceptions relative to the key issues being discussed.

Another issue is whether to make groups relatively homogeneous or relatively heterogeneous. In general, heterogeneity is probably to be preferred, with one critical exception. For some topics, the difference in background or experience may be so salient as to make it uncomfortable for people to speak candidly. For example, if the topic is anti-Semitism, the dynamics of the group would almost certainly be different if the groups consisted of all Jews or all non-Jews, or instead were mixed. From the point of view of designing questions to measure experiences that Jewish respondents perceived as anti-Semitic, it probably would be best to talk with Jews in a context where they did not have to worry about how what they said would appear to a non-Jew, and vice versa.

On the other hand, sometimes mixing is better. In a study of medical treatment choices, putting patients who choose surgical and nonsurgical options in the same group may highlight the differences in their concerns and the weights they gave to different consequences. However, the differences among those who chose the same treatment may be less evident; those differences might be better illuminated in a group made up of people who all chose the same treatment.

The composition of the group will affect what is learned. On a particular topic, researchers may want to try some homogeneous groups and some mixed groups with respect to a particular topic. The results may be different but equally valuable.

The way to organize a focus group for question design and evaluation is essentially the way a survey instrument would be designed. A draft survey instrument constitutes a good protocol for a focus group discussion.

There are three basic topics of conversation in a focus group devoted to an interview schedule. An interview schedule consists of a set of questions about a series of experiences, behaviors, or subjective states. The research questions are three:

1. Are the questions appropriately covering what respondents are supposed to describe?
2. Are the response tasks that questions will pose tasks that respondents are able and willing to perform?
3. Do the words or descriptions proposed in the questions convey consistent meaning, so that people will have a common understanding of what question they are to answer?

Let us go back to the example of measuring people's participation in art-related events. A series of discussion questions might be something like the following:

1. First, we are going to ask people about attendance in the last year at classical music performances. What are some of the kinds of things you have gone to in the past year that might count?

Note: Whenever someone suggests a kind of event that might be borderline, encourage the group to give feedback on whether there is or is not agreement about whether or not that should be included.

2. The question is going to ask people to report the number of times in the past year they have attended a classical music performance. Can you answer that question?

2a. What if we gave you some categories, instead of asking you to give an exact number? For example, what if we used categories such as not at all, 1 to 5 times, 6 to 10 times, or more than 10 times? How well do you think you could perform that task?

3. A key term here is classical music. You have given us some examples of experiences that you think might count as classical music performances. Could we talk a bit about what does and does not count as classical music, as you understand the term?

It probably is typical for focus group discussions to go from general concepts to specifics. A critical step before starting a focus group about a survey instrument is to make a list of the realities, recall tasks, reporting tasks, and terms that are most critical to include. Groups should specifically be asked to share their experiences and perceptions with respect to these flagged issues, as well as other issues that come up in the course of the group discussion.

Using Focus Group Results

One commonly expressed concern about the value of focus groups is that the results are diffuse and hard to work with. Like most research results, the key to value is having a clear set of objectives. When the goal of a focus group discussion is to aid in the design and evaluation of survey questions, and if the focus group discussion is undertaken at the time that there is at least a draft of a survey instrument, the product of the focus group discussion should be a question-by-question review of the survey instrument that is drafted.

1. In light of the range of things that group members had do say, does the researcher want to revise the objectives of the questions, the realities about which respondents will be asked?

2. Can all, or almost all, the respondents perform the response tasks posed by the question? If not, in what way can the response task be revised (shortening the reporting period, increasing the size of response categories, changing the response scale) so that all or most respondents can perform the task more easily?

3. Are all the terms and concepts in the questions well defined so that respondents will consistently know what they are supposed to report? If not, what was learned about the ambiguities or imprecisions of question wording that could be used to write clearer questions?

A basic first step is to have a record of what was said in a focus group. Having the leader take notes is a poor idea. Leaders have too much to do running the group. A better alternative is to have one or more observers take notes. One-way windows, so observers do not intrude on the group process, are good for this purpose.

The best strategy is probably to videotape the groups. In that way, several people involved in a project can watch the tape together, discuss the results, and replay key parts as needed. The impact of a videotape on viewers is much greater than that of an audio tape, and the videotaping process is quite unintrusive to participants. Audio taping is an alternative that records the content of the discussion. However, because it often is hard to identify speakers, it is a somewhat less effective way to capture what occurs.

Focused discussion groups are an extraordinarily efficient way to obtain a great deal of information relevant to the design of survey questions. People with no previous experience with focus groups are routinely amazed at how much they can learn about the subject they are studying and how to ask questions. The level of investment is so small, compared to the effort involved in most surveys, and the payoff so big, it is hard to explain why every survey does not begin with some focus group discussions.

Having said that, of course a focus group discussion is only the beginning of the process. It helps lay out a range of problems that a good survey instrument will have to solve, and it is a beginning to solving some of the vocabulary and conceptual problems. However, intensive individual interviews and field pretests are necessary to examine some aspects of survey questions that cannot be addressed in a focus group discussion.

INTENSIVE INDIVIDUAL INTERVIEWS

As previously mentioned, in the early 1980s, survey researchers and cognitive psychologists met to discuss their mutual interests. One key conclusion was that question testing should include procedures routinely used by cognitive psychologists to learn what respondents are thinking when they are trying to answer questions. Prior to that conference, researchers such as Belson (1981) had "debriefed" respondents about their understanding of questions. However, it probably is fair to trace the current interest in the cognitive laboratory interview to the impetus from the conference (Jabine, Straf, & Tanur, 1984) and to the pioneering work at the National Center for Health Statistics (Lessler, 1987; Lessler & Tourangeau, 1989).

Although cognitive or intensive interviews take several forms and shapes, there are some common elements that define them (Forsyth & Lessler, 1991):

1. The priority of the process is to find out how respondents understand questions and perform the response tasks; there is no particular effort to replicate the data collection procedures to be used in the full-scale survey.

2. Respondents often are brought into a special setting in which interviews can be recorded and observed. Hence, they often are referred to as "laboratory interviews."

3. In contrast to field pretests that utilize survey interviewers, the people who conduct cognitive interviews usually are not regular survey interviewers. Sometimes they are cognitive psychologists; sometimes they are members of the research staff; sometimes they are senior supervisors of interviewing staffs. In all cases, however, they are thoroughly familiar with the objectives of the research and of individual questions so that they can be sensitive to discrepancies between the way respondents perform their tasks and what researchers envision as the way the tasks will be performed.

4. Most critically, the basic protocol involves reading questions to respondents, having them answer the questions, and then some strategy for finding out what was going on in the respondents' minds during the question-and-answer process.

The selection of respondents, people to be interviewed in this process, is parallel to the selection criteria for setting up focus groups. The goal is to get a set of people representative of the range of individuals who will be interviewed in the actual survey. Because special demands are made on respondents, they usually are paid. Sessions tend to last an hour to an hour and a half; beyond two hours, most researchers have found that the ability of respondents to tolerate the task is exhausted. Because the interaction is time consuming, interviews usually cannot cover more than 15 or 20 minutes worth of survey questions. It is common for these laboratory interviews to cover only a sample of questions in a proposed survey interview.

There are three common procedures for trying to monitor the cognitive processes of the respondent who is answering questions (Forsyth & Lessler, 1991).

1. "Think-aloud" interviews
2. Asking probe or follow-up questions after each question or short series of questions.
3. Going through the questions twice, first having respondents answer them in the usual way, then returning to the questions and having a discussion with respondents about the response tasks.

"Think-aloud" interviews are a common technique for cognitive psychologists. In essence, respondents are trained to think out loud, to try to articulate their thoughts and their cognitive processes as they absorb a question, search their memories for information required by the question, and turn the information they have into an answer. When this is done well, it provides a good window into how questions are being understood and answers are being generated. On the negative side, respondents vary in how well they can perform this task. Some respondents have a great deal of difficulty verbalizing their cognitive processes. People with more formal education may do better than others. Also, the form in which information about cognitive processes is gleaned from this process is not structured. Hence, it may place extra demands on the interviewer or people observing the interview to reach conclusions about question problems. Finally, some people are concerned that the think-aloud process itself affects the way respondents address answering questions.

Probably a more commonly used strategy is to ask respondents questions about the question-and-answer process. A standard protocol might be to read a question, have the respondent go through the process of answering the question, and then ask a series of questions to the respondent about the task. Common techniques include:

1. asking respondents to paraphrase their understanding of the question.
2. asking respondents to define terms.
3. asking respondents for any uncertainties or confusions they had about what the appropriate answer was.
4. asking respondents how confident they are that they can give an accurate answer.
5. if the question called for a numerical figure, asking respondents how they arrived at the number; if a question calls for a rating task, asking respondents to talk about the process they went through to decide on the answer.

As noted above, this process can be done in one of two ways. First, respondents can be taken through the cognitive protocol after each question or series of questions. Second, the interviewer can go through the entire interview, then go back through the questions with the cognitive protocol. The advantage of the former approach is that when questions follow immediately after the respondent went through the cognitive task, it is easier for respondents to talk about their thought processes. On the other hand, such a protocol breaks up the interview and any relationship that may exist among questions. For that reason, the interview process itself may be less realistic. When respondents are asked to revisit questions, going back through the interview schedule, they can describe their understanding of questions and elaborate on their answers, but, of course, it is unrealistic to think they can reconstruct their thought process at the time they originally answered the questions.

Like focus groups, cognitive interviews are best and most productive if a specific objectives and concerns have been laid out. Researchers should flag particular issues with respect to vocabulary, comprehension, and forming a response that they consider potentially problematic. Then, along with more general questions about comprehension and difficulty, the interviewer specifically probes the respondents with respect to the issues identified in advance. An example of a protocol for a cognitive interview is presented in Figure 5.1.

Although the objectives and the products of these intensive interviews may seem similar to those of the focus groups, cognitive interviews are complementary to focus groups. The great advantage of focus groups is that they are efficient; the perceptions and experiences of seven or eight people can be garnered in an hour and a half. In contrast, the intensive individual interviews produce the experience of only one person in an hour and a half. On the other hand, focus groups do not provide good tests of the specific wording of individual questions. Wording can be discussed, but that is not the same as finding out how a person processes a set of specific words. In a similar way, people in groups can discuss how they could or would answer questions, but it is not possible to replicate the actual answer formation process that respondents have to go through. In both cases, researchers are attempting to understand problems that will affect consistent understanding of questions and the ability of respondents to answer questions in a consistent and accurate way. However, focus groups attack these problems in a general way, whereas intensive individual interviews are designed to look at the specific problems of comprehension and the response experience.

There are some aspects of good question design that neither focus groups nor intensive individual interviews will address. First, neither

A1.   How many days in the past 30 days did you feel sexual *drive*?

       _____ days

A2.   Have you felt your sexual *drive* in the past month to be:

      [ ]   MUCH MORE THAN USUAL
      [ ]   SOMEWHAT MORE THAN USUAL
      [ ]   USUAL
      [ ]   SOMEWHAT LESS THAN USUAL
      [ ]   MUCH LESS THAN USUAL

A3. Have you felt your sexual *interest* in the past month to be:

      [ ]   MUCH MORE THAN USUAL
      [ ]   SOMEWHAT MORE THAN USUAL
      [ ]   USUAL
      [ ]   SOMEWHAT LESS THAN USUAL
      [ ]   MUCH LESS THAN USUAL

(Now I'm going to ask some specific things about how you answered those questions.)

    a.   Would you summarize in your own words what you think the term sexual *drive* meant?
    b.   In what ways, if any, does the term sexual *interest* mean something different?
    c.   Tell me how you went about calculating the answer you gave for the frequency of sexual drive?
    d.   When you were asked to compare your interest and desire now with "usual," what did you think of as "usual"? (When was that?) (What made you choose that as usual?)

Figure 5.1. Cognitive Protocol

tests whether or not a question is easy and comfortable for interviewers to read as written. To find that out, questions need to be tested by a sample of interviewers under realistic conditions. How well a supervisor reads questions in a laboratory setting is not an indication of how interviewers will actually read the question in people's homes or on the telephone.

Second, tasks that paid volunteers are able and willing to do under laboratory conditions may not be the same as when respondents are interrupted in the middle of their day-to-day lives to be interview respondents. Questions that are clearly problematic under laboratory conditions will almost certainly be problematic under normal survey interview conditions as well; the opposite may not be the case (Royston, 1989; Willis, Royston, & Bercini, 1989). For that reason, after the focus groups and the intensive individual interviews, it is necessary to test survey questions under realistic data collection procedures.

FIELD PRETESTING

There is a prototype of a traditional field pretest for interviewer-administered surveys. When a survey instrument is in near final form, experienced interviewers conduct 15 to 35 interviews with people similar to those who will be respondents in a planned survey. Data collection procedures are designed to be similar to those to be used in the planned survey, except that people interviewed are likely to be chosen on the basis of convenience and availability, rather than by some probability sampling strategy. Question evaluation from such a survey mainly comes from interviewers (Converse & Presser, 1986).

Most often interviewers meet with investigators to discuss their pretest experience. Interviewers report on practical problems, such as typographical errors, faulty instructions about skipping questions, and inadequate arrangements for recording answers. Researchers also find out how long interviews take.

Gaining information about such practical issues is an essential step prior to carrying out a full-scale survey. Interviewers also are asked to report on questions that they see as posing problems for them or for their respondents. Unfortunately as mechanisms for systematic evaluation of survey questions, such pretests as traditionally carried out have some significant limitations (Presser, 1989). These include:

1. The criteria for question evaluation often are not well articulated; even when they are, interviewers are likely to differ in their perceptions of what constitutes a question problem.

2. The ability of interviewers to diagnose questions is confounded by two other factors as well. First, it is difficult to be put in the dual role of both attempting to carry out a good interview and being an observer of the interview. Second, interviewers are selected and trained to be good problem solvers. Good interviewers can read poorly written questions as worded, and they are good at probing to elicit adequate answers even when questions are poorly designed. Because of their skills, senior interviewers are likely not to be sensitive to the question problems that they are successful in solving.

3. Interviewers in pretests have small samples of respondents. When a respondent has a problem with a question, there is a judgment to be made about whether the fault lies with the respondent's idiosyncrasies or with the question. If a question is problematic for 20% or 40% of the sample, that constitutes a serious problem. Yet, that may mean that an interviewer who takes only half a dozen pretest interviews may have only a single respondent who had difficulty with the question.

4. Debriefing sessions may not be a good way to get information about interviewer evaluations. Inevitably, some interviewers speak out more often and eloquently than others, not necessarily in proportion to the quality of the things they have to say.
5. Some question problems may not be apparent in the course of a pretest interview. An important reason for focus groups and particularly cognitive interviews prior to a pretest is to identify comprehension problems in advance. However, pretests with larger and possibly more representative samples of respondents potentially could provide another opportunity for identifying difficulties in question comprehension. However, although some such problems may be apparent to interviewers, others may not be without special steps.

Recently, there has been an effort to develop strategies for strengthening the traditional pretest to address some of these problems. The specific techniques that warrant the most attention are:

1. Systematic coding of interviewer and respondent behavior during the pretest interview (Morton-Williams & Sykes, 1984; Oksenberg, Cannell, & Kalton, 1991).
2. The use of systematic rating forms by interviewers to evaluate questions.
3. The use of special probes for debriefing respondents to pretest interviews.

Coding Interviewer and Respondent Behavior

The basic technique is straightforward. Pretest interviews are tape recorded. This can be done in person or over the telephone. For telephone interviews, it is important to inform respondents explicitly that the interview is being tape recorded and to get their permission for that, in order not to break any laws. It has been well established that respondents seldom decline to have interviews tape recorded if the idea is properly presented (Fowler & Mangione, 1990).

The tape recordings are then coded as an aid to evaluating questions. Several different coding schemes have been used. An example of a form used for such an evaluation is presented as Figure 5.2. The basic approaches are all consistent.

1. The way that interviewers read the question is evaluated. For each question, a coder uses one of three codes: (a) the question was read exactly as worded, (b) the question was read with only minor changes that did not affect the meaning, or (c) the question was altered in some significant way,

Instructions to coders: Write down every question number on the lines provided in the "QUESTION" column on the form below (treating questions with an introductory stem as a separate "question.")

If a question is correctly skipped, mark the first column. If the question is correctly read, put a mark in the second column "NO ERRORS." You may hear 2 different types of reading errors: major and minor. A minor reading error is when the interviewer reads the question slightly differently from how it is written, but does *not* change the meaning of the question. For example, the interviewer leaves out the article, "a" or "the." A major reading error is when the interviewer reads the question differently from the way it is written and *changes* the meaning of the question. Another reading error that is considered major is the situation of a question that has an introductory stem and the interviewer fails to read the stem for the required amount of items (i.e. the interviewer is supposed to read the stem for at least the first three items, but only reads it for the first on, or the interviewer omits one or more response alternatives).

The "INTERRUPTION" column is used when respondents give an answer before the question is completely read to them.

The "REPEAT QUESTION" column is for recording the number of times the interviewer repeats all or part of the question.

The "OTHER PROBES" column is to record the number of times the interviewer uses other probes to get an answer.

The "R ASKS FOR CLARIFICATION" column is used if the respondent asks for clarification, "what do you mean?," or the respondent doesn't know the meaning of a word.

READING

Question	Correct Skip	No Errors	Minor Errors	Major Errors	Interrupt	Repeat Question	Other Probes	R Asks for Clarification
A1								
A1A								
A2								
A3								
A4								
A4A								
A5								

Figure 5.2. Behavior Coding

either by changing the wording in a way that affected the meaning or leaving out some significant words in the question.

2. The respondent interrupted the reading of the question, either by asking a question or attempting to provide an answer before the question had been read in its entirety.

3. The initial response of the respondent was inadequate; the answer did not meet the question objectives. To improve the answer, the interviewer:

   (a) Repeated the question

   (b) Used some other kind of follow-up probe to the respondent's initial answer in order to get an answer that met the question objectives.

4. The respondent asks for clarification of the question. This code is used any time a respondent asks the interviewer anything about the question itself prior to answering it.

The rationale behind coding the behavior in pretest interviews is the following: When a survey interview is going perfectly, the interviewer will read the question exactly as written once, after which the respondent will give an answer that meets the question objectives. When there are deviations from this, the perfect question-and-answer process, it may be an indication of a question problem. The more often deviations occur, the more likely there is to be a problem with the question.

It turns out that questions have reliable, predictable effects on the behavior of respondents and interviewers. In one study, the same survey instrument was pretested by two different survey organizations. The results of the behavior coding of the pretests were then compared question by question. It was found that the rate at which three key behaviors occurred—reading questions exactly as worded, respondent requests for clarification, and respondents providing inadequate answers to questions—were highly and significantly correlated between the two pretests. Thus, regardless of who does the interviewing, the same questions are likely to produce misread questions, requests for clarification, and inadequate answers.

The product of the behavior coding is a simple distribution for each question. From the coding, the rate at which each of the behaviors occurred across all the pretest interviews is tabulated. The results of the tabulation might look something like the output presented in Figure 5.3.

If questions that are difficult to read can be identified during the pretest stage, they can be rewritten. One of the best ways to have interviewers administer survey instruments in a standardized way is to give them questions that they are able and willing to read as written.

READING

Ques-tion	Correct Skip	No Errors	Minor Errors	Major Errors	Inter-rupt	Repeat Ques-tion	Other Probes	R Asks for Clarifi-cation
A1		22	2	1				
A1A		25				1	8	
A2		25				5	1	1
A3		22	3				1	
A4		9	11	6		1	1	3
A4A		21	3	1				1
A5		24			1			5

Figure 5.3. Compiled Behavior Coding Form

Interrupted questions, requests for clarification and inadequate answers are significant for three reasons. First, they can be indicators of questions that are unclear or not consistently understood by respondents. Second, they can be indicators of questions that do not clearly specify the kind of answer that will meet the question objectives. Third, any time a respondent fails to answer directly, it requires interviewers to exercise judgment. The more often interviewers are required to solve problems before an answer is obtained, the more likely they are to influence answers and the less standardized the data collection (Fowler & Mangione, 1990; Mangione, Fowler, & Louis, 1992).

When a respondent interrupts the reading of a question, the interviewer has a decision to make. Good survey practice requires that a respondent hear the entire question before providing an answer. However, if the interviewer thinks the answer provided is probably the right one, the answer may simply be accepted. Alternatively, the interviewer may go back and decide to read either the entire question again or the part of the question that was not read to the respondent prior to accepting an answer. From the point of view of standardized measurement, it is best if questions are designed so that interruptions are minimal, so that interviewers less frequently have to make those choices.

Procedures for behavior coding pretest interviews have been shown to be quite easy and efficient. Coding does not require any particular background or experience; coders can be trained in a few hours. The coding process itself can be done almost at the rate of the interview, without stopping the tape recorder very often. Although tabulation can be facilitated by designing a direct data entry system on a computer, hand tabulations such as those illustrated in Figure 5.3 are perfectly satisfactory.

The strengths of behavior coding results are that they are objective, systematic, replicable, and quantitative. Interviewers cannot have a real quantitative sense for how often they encounter respondents who have difficulty with questions. Indeed, interviewers are not even very good at identifying questions that they do not read exactly as written. Hence, behavior coding adds considerably to the information researchers have about their questions.

The quantifiable nature of the results provides perspective by allowing comparison of how frequently problems occur across questions and across surveys. It also constitutes more credible evidence to researchers of the presence of a problem with a question. When interviewers say that they think that respondents are having difficulty with a question, it is hard for researchers to know how much weight to give that perception. When the behavior coding shows that 25% of the respondents asked for clarification before they answered a question, the evidence is clearer that something should be done.

Once the data have been tabulated, the next issue is how best to use the results. One issue is when the rate of a problem is high enough that it constitutes a question problem. Although a guideline cutpoint of 15% has been used (Oksenberg et al., 1991), clearly that is somewhat arbitrary. However, it has been found that when one of these behaviors occurs in at least 15% of pretest interviews, it is likely that there is an identifiable problem with a question that could be improved. In the example in Figure 5.3, questions A1A, A2, and A5 all look as if they have potential problems based on the amount of probing interviewers did and the requests for clarification. Question A4 clearly poses a reading problem and perhaps a response problem.

Although a notable rate of one or more of these behaviors is an indication that a problem exists, further steps are needed to identify the nature of the problem. Using the experience of the interviewers and the people who coded the behaviors can be helpful.

Research organizations differ in the way in which they use these data. One common strategy is to include data from the behavior coding of the pretest interviews in the interviewer debriefing session after a pretest. In the course of discussing individual questions, if a problem was apparent in the behavior coding, interviewers can be asked to give their analysis of what it is about the question that caused the problem. Why is this question difficult to read as worded? What sorts of problems were respondents having in providing adequate answers?

The people doing the behavior coding can be included in that same session, or they can have a separate debriefing of their own. The goal at this stage should be to learn as much as possible about the nature of the problems with the questions, so input from both interviewers and coders should be part of the question evaluation process.

There is the issue about how to solve the problem. In some cases, the solution is obvious and easy. If there is a term that respondents do not consistently understand, the solution typically is to define the term. If interviewers are not reading a dangling modifying clause at the end of a question, the solution is probably to move the clause or drop it. Figure 5.4 provides a list of some common question flaws that show up in behavior coding to which researchers might want to attend. There is overlap between this list and the principles listed in Chapter 4.

Finally, once researchers have collected information about questions, attempted to analyze the nature of the problem, and come up with a solution, there is really only one way to find out if the process was successful in producing a better question: Do another pretest, evaluate the questions in the same way, and see if things work better.

Question Rating Forms for Interviewers

The traditional way of obtaining information from interviewers about survey questions is to have a meeting after the pretest interviews are completed at which interviewers share their perceptions and experiences with the survey questions. Certainly, it is critical for any researcher to obtain feedback about ways in which a survey instrument poses problems for interviewers. However, the criteria interviewers use to evaluate questions are likely to vary from interviewer to interviewer, and a group discussion is not a very systematic way to elicit people's views.

In an effort to improve the value of what pretest interviewers contribute to the question evaluation process, researchers recently have been experimenting with having interviewers fill out systematic ratings of each question. An example of such a form is presented as Figure 5.5.

The form is quite straightforward. Question numbers are listed down the side. Interviewers are asked to make three ratings of each question:

Behavior	Common Problems
Interviewers misread questions	Awkward wording (hard to say smoothly).
	Introductions that interviewers find superfluous or do not fit context.
	Dangling clauses at the end of question.
	Missing words to set up the response task.
Interruptions	Dangling modifying clauses after a complete question has been asked.
	Respondent does not realize there will be response alternatives given.
Interviewer probing (or inadequate answers)	Meaning of question is unclear.
	Unclear, undefined terms.
	Unclear response task
	Poor question order, so respondent cannot recall response alternatives.
Request for clarification	Unclear, undefined terms.
	Unclear response task.
	Poor question order, so respondents cannot recall response alternatives.

Figure 5.4. Common Question Problems That Affect Respondent and Interviewer Behavior

1. To what extent, if any, is there difficulty in reading the question exactly as worded?
2. To what extent, if any, does the question contain words or concepts that are not easily or consistently understood by respondents?
3. To what extent, if any, do respondents have difficulty in knowing or providing the answer to the question?

The rating scheme used in this particular form is very simple. It asks interviewers to rate the question as an (A) no apparent problem, (B) a possible problem, or (C) a definite problem.

The suggested protocol for use of this form is as follows. When interviewers do a pretest interview, they make notes to themselves in the margin when they notice a problem along any of the lines covered by the ratings. After the interview is over, they transfer the notes, with elaborations, into a master interview schedule. When they follow this process after each pretest interview, the master interview schedule contains all their notes about the problems they observed during the

You are to evaluate each question based on your pretest experience, by writing a code in each of the first three columns for each question.

Use the following code for each potential problem:

A = No evidence of problem
B = Possible problem
C = Definite problem

COLUMN 1 Should be used for potential problems resulting from your having *trouble reading the question as written*

COLUMN 2 Should be used for potential problems resulting from *respondent not understanding words or ideas in the question*

COLUMN 3 Should be used for potential problems resulting from *respondents having trouble providing answer to question*

Question	Hard to Read	R Has Problem Under- standing	R Has Trouble Providing Answer	Other Problems	Comments
A1	A	A	A		
A1A	B	A	A		
A2	A	B	A		
A3	A	A	A		
A4	C	C	B		
A4A	A	A	B		
A5	A	A	A		

Figure 5.5. Interviewer Rating Form

pretest. Then, armed with that master form, they fill out the ratings of each question prior to the interviewer debriefing session.

These rating forms actually serve three different functions:

1. The most obvious and undeniable value of the forms is that they provide a handy way for researchers to tabulate the initial perceptions of the interviewers about question problems.
2. The forms also ensure that researchers have access to the opinions of all the interviewers in evaluating questions, not just those who speak up in debriefing sessions.

3. The rating forms focus interviewer attention on the critical aspects of survey questions, aspects that sometimes are not the main focus of interviewer attention.

Analysis of what interviewers say in debriefing sessions suggests they usually focus on the things about the interview schedule that cause problems for them: faulty skips, inadequate space to record answers, and wordy questions. These practical aspects of the survey instrument often dominate the conversation in debriefing sessions after pretests. In essence, this particular rating form asks interviewers to provide systematic input on some aspects of the survey instrument that may not be real problems for interviewers but that are of critical importance to the quality of measurement.

If interviewers complete these rating forms prior to the debriefing session, the person leading the session can have summaries of their question evaluations available at the time questions are discussed. A fourth benefit of having these rating forms is that it makes it possible to focus the conversation in the debriefing on those questions that interviewers consider most problematic.

It is likely that forms even better and more useful than the one in Figure 5.5 can be developed. However, the optimal form probably will not be much more complicated. When more complex forms were tried, it took more interviewer effort without increasing the value of the ratings. The goal of the ratings should be to flag problem questions; diagnosing the nature of the problem is done better in a discussion.

The cost of having interviewers complete such a form is very small. Given the benefits outlined above, it is difficult to argue against the value of using some such rating form as one part of the question evaluation and pretest process.

Special Questions for Respondents

The principal goal of a standard pretest is to evaluate a near-final survey instrument. To do that, we usually want to replicate as closely as possible the way interviews will be conducted in the full-scale survey.

As we have discussed above, that question-and-answer process in a standardized survey does not always provide a window into how respondents understand questions and what their answers mean. The main reason for advocating the use of focus groups and, particularly, intensive laboratory interviews prior to field pretesting is to identify as many cognitive problems as possible before the field pretest. In addition, the behavior coding described above will provide indications of some questions that are not understood in a consistent way. Nonetheless, we know some respondents will answer questions adequately, without asking for clarification, when in fact their understanding of the question is imperfect. For this reason, researchers have been interested in developing other ways of using pretests to more perfectly identify questions that are understood inconsistently by respondents.

Normally, researchers are reluctant to add very many questions to a regular pretest for two different reasons. First, if extra questions or demands are made on respondents during the interview itself, it changes the dynamics of the interview as well as its length, which may reduce the ability of researchers to have a realistic test of how their survey instrument will work. Second, assuming that a survey is relying on volunteer respondents, as is almost always the case, there probably are limits to the willingness of respondents to take time to help evaluate questions, in addition to serving as pretest respondents.

Within those limits, researchers have explored at least three different approaches to having pretest respondents further assist in the process of question evaluation.

1. Respondents can be asked to describe the way they understood particular questions. The techniques used in cognitive interviews, to ask respondents to paraphrase questions or to provide definitions of key terms or concepts, both can be used to attempt to identify places where respondent understanding of questions is imperfect.

2. In a similar way, respondents can be asked to explain in more detail the basis on which they formed an answer to a question. That is particularly appropriate when the question calls for a fixed response, a choice among answers provided in the interview schedule. It often is instructive to have the respondent elaborate in narrative form on the answers to such questions, so the researchers can evaluate how well the chosen answer reflects what the respondent had to say.

3. Respondents can be asked for their evaluations of different question properties. Two common evaluations are to ask respondents how accurately they were able to answer certain questions and how likely they think they or others would be to distort answers to certain questions.

Comprehension Probes

Example 5.1: In the past month, how many times have you seen or talked with a medical doctor about your health?

This question is designed to include telephone conversations with physicians, as well as office visits. It is intended to cover all kinds of medical specialties, including psychiatrists. Researchers might wonder whether or not respondents understood the scope of the question in the way it was intended. A series of follow-up questions might be asked as follows:

Example 5.1:

a. Did the number you gave me include any occasions when you obtained medical advice from a physician on the telephone, rather than seeing the physician in person?
b. In the last month, were there any occasions when you talked with a physician on the telephone about your health?
c. If you had talked with a physician about your health on the telephone during the past month, do you think you would have reported it in answer to that question?
d. Did the number you gave me include any visits to a psychiatrist?
e. In the past month, did you have any visits to psychiatrists?
f. If you had visited a psychiatrist in the past month, do you think you would have reported it in response to that question?

Example 5.2: In the past month, on about how many days did you do any kind of physical exercise for at least 20 minutes?

Follow-up questions could look something like the following:

Example 5.2a: When you were counting up the times when you exercised, did you include walking for exercise at all?

Example 5.2b: In the past month, on how many days, if any, did you walk for exercise for at least 20 minutes?

Example 5.2c: If you had walked for exercise in the past month, do you think you would have reported in answer to this question?

There are several points to be made about how to use a series like this. First, obviously it requires that the researcher have a specific focus of attention. Experience shows that general fishing excursions for ambiguities are not very productive. These questions work best when they are aimed at a particular concern about comprehension.

The entire series is valuable because each question gives different information. The first two questions are mutually dependent, and both are needed to give perspective on the significance of the other answer. The first question gives an estimate of the frequency with which the events are included; the second question gives a reading on how frequently the focus events are missed or omitted.

The significance of the answer to the third question needs to be treated with caution. The answers to hypothetical questions are often unreliable. Nonetheless, if a significant number of people appear to misunderstand the question, even in a hypothetical sense, it argues that the researcher may want to work on the definitions in the question.

Using Narrative Answers

In a recent survey, respondents were asked how many novels they had read in the past year. Researchers wondered if respondents knew what a novel was.

To evaluate that in the pretest, respondents were asked the following:

Example 5.3: You said that in the past year you had read about (NUMBER) novels. I wonder if you could tell me the names of some of the novels that you have read.

The answers then were coded as to whether or not they were novels. The results showed that about 25% of the books that respondents thought were novels in fact were nonfiction.

All of the above examples referred to factual questions, questions for which in theory there were right or wrong answers. The goal of the probing was to find out whether people had a shared understanding of questions and answers, so that the answers could be interpreted as the researchers wanted to interpret them. The same kind of technique can be used for more subjective ratings.

Example 5.4: Overall, how would you rate your health—excellent, very good, good, fair, or poor?

Example 5.4a: When you said that your health was (PREVIOUS ANSWER), what did you take into account or think about in making that rating?

In this case the goal of the question is to get a rating of health status, how healthy the person is. When the probe outlined above was asked, it was learned that people used a variety of criteria for assessing their health. For example, some people based their rating on how healthy they considered their lifestyle. They would say they rated their health only "fair" because they were not exercising regularly or eating as well as they should. Others seemed to be rating primarily their fitness, rather than the presence of any conditions that might affect their function or their longevity.

For some purposes, rating the healthiness of one's lifestyle is very different from rating one's health status. As a result of this follow-up question, researchers learned that if they wanted respondents to use the same criteria for rating their health, they had to do a better job of explaining what dimension respondents were supposed to be using.

Asking respondents to evaluate questions is a third approach to evaluating questions. One of the most interesting and successful uses of such questions is found in the work of Bradburn, Sudman, and associates (1979). Their basic interview covered a series of activities, such as drinking to excess, sexual activities, income, and education. In their respondent debriefings after the interview, they asked three different kinds of questions. First, they asked whether any of the questions were too hard or difficult. Then they asked whether any of the questions were too personal. Third, they asked how respondents thought most people would feel about answering the questions—very uneasy, moderately uneasy, slightly uneasy, or not at all uneasy.

Their conclusion was that asking people whether they found questions hard or personal were themselves threatening questions. Our research has yielded much the same conclusion. For the most part, we do not think we get helpful information from respondents when they are asked directly the extent to which questions are hard or personal for them.

On the other hand, Bradburn and Sudman found the answers to the projective questions, the ones about how respondents thought other people would feel about questions, to be informative and to conform better to information they had about response error.

One could argue that this is an example of asking people questions to which they do not know the answers. However, the projective assumption is that people identify with others when they answer a question like this, and they really are telling researchers how they themselves feel about the questions.

Conclusion

The focus of this section is on the potential to bring some of the techniques from the cognitive laboratory out into a realistic survey setting, so that feedback can be obtained from a larger, more representative sample of respondents under more realistic data collection conditions. In order to keep such probing from interfering with the primary goal of the pretest, probing questions have to be fairly limited. The best strategy is probably to focus on half a dozen questions. After an interview is over, interviewers can go back to those questions, remind respondents of what the questions were, and then ask follow-up questions of the sorts outlined above. As noted, the more focused and explicit the goals of these follow-up questions, the more likely they are to serve the purpose for which they are intended.

If such limited evaluation is not sufficient, and there are objectives that cannot realistically be achieved in a laboratory setting, some researchers may want to consider a hybrid strategy, which some researchers call an "in-depth interview." In essence, in-depth interviews bring some of the elements of the cognitive laboratory into more realistic survey settings. Specially trained interviewers ask detailed follow-up questions about many questions in a survey. Interviews typically are done in people's homes. Samples are larger and more representative than can usually be produced in cognitive laboratories. When such in-depth interviews are done, it adds another step to the question development and evaluation process. Subsequently, researchers still need to produce a near-final survey instrument to be subjected to a full field pretest.

Once a survey instrument is ready for a field pretest, most of the questions about comprehension of questions and the cognitive aspects of the response tasks should have been resolved. However, when a field pretest is done, the possibility of asking a few follow-up questions after the pretest interview is complete is one more opportunity for the researcher to evaluate the cognitive aspects of a few questions before committing to a full-scale survey.

ADAPTING PRETEST STRATEGIES TO
SELF-ADMINISTERED QUESTIONNAIRES

The above strategies, particularly behavior coding and systematic interviewer ratings, depend on the fact that the question-and-answer process is carried out orally in an interviewer-administered survey. In contrast, when self-administered questionnaires are used, all of the key question-and-answer behavior takes place inside a respondent's head. The same issues of course are relevant. Respondents have to understand questions in a consistent way, they have to understand what answers meet the question objectives, and they have to be able to perform the response tasks. The issue addressed in this section is how to adapt the procedures discussed above to the special requirements and challenges of self-administration.

The first point to be made is that focus groups and cognitive interviews can be utilized as well for self-administered forms as for interviewer-administered forms. Questions to be asked in self-administered form specifically should be subjected to cognitive laboratory techniques, wherein questions are asked orally and answers are given orally.

A distinctive feature of self-administered questionnaires, compared to interviews, is that respondents are looking at all the response alternatives. Hence, a realistic way to carry out the intensive cognitive interviews may be to have respondents looking at a version of the questions they are asked, so that they see the response alternatives they will be offered. However, carrying out the question-and-answer process orally gives the interviewer access to much more information about what is going on in the respondent's head.

Once there is a near-final survey instrument that has been subjected to these various kinds of evaluations, there still is a need to do a pretest to evaluate how the question-and-answer process goes. Obviously, interviewer evaluation does not fit this protocol. However, observation of respondents filling out the questionnaires and debriefing respondents about the questions are appropriate options for self-administered surveys.

Field Pretest Without Observation

One obvious way to pretest a mail survey procedure is to replicate the mail survey: Questionnaires can be mailed to people, who can be asked to fill them out and can return them by mail. In addition, respondents may be asked to answer a few debriefing questions. For example, at the end of the instrument, respondents might be asked to identify any questions they found confusing, that they had difficulty answering, or that for other reasons posed problems.

Like its counterpart in the traditional field pretest of an interviewer-administered survey, such a field pretest does not provide very much information about the question-and-answer process. Written notes from pretest respondents may be better than nothing, but probably not much better. The criteria they use are likely to be hard to define, and in general we know that respondents are not very good critics of survey questions.

Thus, although such a pretest may provide information about willingness to return the questionnaire, ability to get through it, and perhaps some information about how long it takes to fill out the instrument (assuming there is a question about that), other steps are needed to find out about the question-and-answer process.

Using Observation to Evaluate
Self-Administered Questions

Watching people fill out self-administered questionnaires can provide useful information about question problems. If respondents take a long time to answer a question, it may suggest the question is either confusing or hard to answer. To date, there are no reliable studies of the value of observations in identifying problem questions. Moreover, it is a labor-intensive enterprise, because one observer must be assigned to look over the shoulder of each respondent, in order to actually identify questions that take longer than average to answer. Nonetheless, there probably is potential to learn things from such observations, and this is an area in which further research might be valuable.

It is more certain that when questionnaires require respondents to gather information from records or other sources, actually observing the process that respondents go through to obtain the information required can be very informative. The application of this method is probably most relevant in organizational surveys. Frequently, respondents will be asked to gather information about such things as the number of employees in certain job classifications or the quantity of sales in certain areas. It is important that researchers understand how easy or hard their requests for information are, so they can structure a realistic task. Asking pretest respondents if an observer can be present while they fill out the questionnaire, to gain an appreciation of what actually is involved in filling out the instrument, can be a very useful exercise and one that probably should be used more often.

Debriefing Respondents

Probably the most universal strategy for evaluating self-administered questionnaires is to have respondents complete them, then carry out a brief interview with the respondents about the survey instrument. This can be done individually or in groups. The sorts of techniques described for debriefing interview respondents can be used in this context. In addition, respondents can be asked about any problems they had with reading and answering questions.

Conclusion

Although cognitive laboratory testing is valuable for both interviewer- and self-administered survey instruments, perhaps it is distinctively important for self-administered questionnaires because of the difficulty during pretesting of identifying clues to question problems. People who completely misunderstand a question or what it calls for can check a box and move on without any problem being evident. As a result, it is very hard to identify cognitive problems and response problems at the final stages of pretesting a self-administered questionnaire. Thus the final pretests of self-administered questionnaires tend primarily to focus on the practical aspects of the instrument itself: making sure that to the extent possible the task is clear and reasonably easy to do. Nonetheless, at each stage, researchers can provide themselves with opportunities to get a reading on at least the obvious comprehension problems that remain in their questions. Best practice would be at each stage, including the final stage, to at least provide some opportunity for pretest respondents to identify questions that are not consistently and reliably understood.

TABULATING ANSWERS

A final step that researchers can take to help evaluate questions at the pretest stage is to tabulate the distribution of answers that result. If fewer than 20 pretest interviews are done, the value of such tabulations is minimal. However, if 30 or more pretest interviews are done, the tabulations can be informative.

Obviously, the limitation of pretest distributions, in addition to limited numbers, is that typically the samples are not representative. However, assuming that samples are reasonably like the population to be studied, there are at least four kinds of information that can be gleaned from looking at pretest data.

1. Response distributions across subjective scales can provide information about whether the right response alternatives have been offered. Recall that the information value of scales is increased to the extent that respon-

dents are distributed across the continuum. If all respondents give the same answer, the question is providing no information whatsoever. If a question provides two response alternatives and 90% of the respondents give one answer, information is being provided by only about 10% of the respondents. Hence, one use of reviewing pretest response distributions is to identify questions where respondents cluster heavily in one or two categories. For such questions, researchers may consider the possibility of changing the response alternatives to increase the extent to which respondents are distributed on the scale, thereby increasing the amount of information gained from the question. Alternatively, on the basis of the response distributions, they may decide that certain questions are not providing useful information and can be dropped from the survey.

2. In some cases, surveys are constructed so that follow-up questions are asked for people who give a particular response.

Example 5.5: In general, in describing the way you feel about the medical care you receive, would you say you are generally satisfied or generally not satisfied?

Example 5.5a: (IF NOT SATISFIED) What is the main way in which you are not satisfied?

In a pretest, it might be found that very few people give the "not satisfied" response. In that case, the follow-up question will be asked of relatively few people, and it will provide little information. Given that information, several changes are possible.

a. Change the initial question, in an attempt to elicit more "dissatisfied" responses.
b. Ask the follow-up question of a broader sample, or even of all respondents as in Example 5.5b.

Example 5.5b: In what ways, if any, would you say you are dissatisfied with the medical care you receive?

c. Drop the follow-up question altogether.

3. The rates of item nonresponse, the percentage of respondents who do not give an answer at all to questions, is another issue that can be addressed from distributions of pretest answers. In most survey instruments, the rates at which respondents do not give answers is low. However, if there are questions that more than a very few respondents fail to answer, it can lead

researchers to reevaluate the wording of the question, the objective of the question, or, in the extreme case, whether the question should be asked at all.

4. Some analyses of the relationships among questions can also be done from data collected in pretests. Subject to limitations of sample size and representativeness, pretest data can be used to look for redundancy and for inconsistency. If several questions in a survey are aimed at measuring the same thing, it can be informative to cross-tabulate the answers or look at the correlations. If the analyses show that the answers are highly related, it may be possible to drop one of the questions without losing information. Alternatively, if questions thought to be measuring the same thing are not highly related, or if there are major inconsistencies in answers, it indicates that questions are measuring different things. That information may lead the researcher to rewrite one or both questions, to rethink the way what is being measured is conceptualized, or possibly to drop one or another of the questions.

A special use of pretests is to provide information about the answers given to questions that call for narrative (or open-ended) answers. In recent years, the use of questions that respondents answer in their own words has declined dramatically. Open-ended answers can be difficult to code, they pose particular problems for computer-assisted interviewing, and the answers are often diverse, thereby complicating analysis. Nonetheless, researchers still do ask some open-ended questions in surveys, and looking at the answers obtained in pretests can help researchers evaluate those questions.

There are two different ways that pretests can be used in connection with narrative answers. First, by looking at the answers that are obtained, the researcher may be able to detect certain inadequacies of the question as posed. A very common problem, discussed frequently in this text, is a failure to specify adequately the kind of answer that will meet question objectives. Looking at the answers to pretest questions can indicate to researchers whether or not they want to further specify to respondents what sorts of answers, and the level of detail in answers, they would like to obtain.

Second, questions that are answered in narrative form often are asked because the researchers think there is a long list of plausible answers or that they do not know all the answers people may offer. Pretesting a question in open-ended form can provide information about the range of answers that people are likely to give. Based on the pretest, the researcher may conclude that a short list of answers will cover what most people have to say. Hence, the question may be transformed from an open-ended question to a question with a fixed set of response alternatives.

Analyzing response distributions means that researchers have to set up their data entry and coding processes at the time of a pretest. That will require some extra effort. However, if the survey instrument is in near-final form for pretest, the work done to be ready to code and enter responses from the pretest will generally not be wasted; most of it will have to be done anyway in connection with entering the data from the final survey. Hence, for many or most surveys, creating a data file of answers from pretest interviews will entail only minimal additional cost.

The value of the information that can be gained from tabulating pretest answers will vary depending on how well the pretest sample approximates the survey population and how many pretest interviews are done. However, the kind of information outlined above can be quite useful to researchers in final evaluation of their questions. Tabulation of answers focused on the kinds of issues outlined above constitutes one more relatively inexpensive way to gain potentially useful information about the measurement properties of questions.

CONCLUSION

A sensible protocol for the development of a survey instrument prior to virtually any substantial survey would include all of the steps outlined above: focus group discussions, intensive laboratory interviews, field pretests with behavior coding and interviewer rating forms, and tabulations of data from pretest interviews. Moreover, in the ideal, at least two field pretests would be done, the second to make sure the problems identified in the first field pretest had been solved.

Arguments against this kind of question evaluation usually focus on time and money. Certainly the elapsed calendar time for the question design process will be longer if focus groups and cognitive interviews are included than if they are not. However, focus groups and cognitive interviews can be carried out in a few weeks.

The time implications of question testing have less to do with the amount of time it takes to gather information about the questions than the time it takes to design new and better questions when problems are found. For almost any survey, experience shows that each of these steps yields information that will enable researchers to design better questions. When question problems are identified, sometimes it takes time and effort to fix them. Once a researcher thinks the problems are fixed, some further evaluation steps are in order to make sure that the solutions are adequate. Yet it is hard to think of a better way to spend research project time than ensuring that the questions that are asked in a survey are reasonable measures of what the researcher is trying to study.

With respect to the cost, a real virtue of the steps outlined is that they are extraordinarily inexpensive in the context of most survey budgets. Assuming that a survey budget included some kind of pretest, the steps outlined will have a very small percentage impact on total costs.

Another argument that is sometimes advanced against question evaluation procedures prior to a survey is that researchers may not want to change questions. Many survey researchers use questions in surveys that will enable them to compare the resulting data with results of surveys of other populations or surveys at an earlier point in time.

A legitimate concern is that if questions are changed, the potential to compare results is compromised or lost. At the same time, if a question is a poor measure, and if the answers do not validly reflect what the researcher wants to measure, the value of replicating or comparing is considerably diminished. A researcher may decide to retain a question even though it has been shown to have some serious problems from the perspective of how it is understood, how interviewers use it, or how people answer the question. A researcher may decide that the goals of comparability are more important than the limits of the question as a measure. Nonetheless, it seems unlikely that a researcher would not want to evaluate the quality of a question in a way such that the decision about keeping or changing a question could be based on the best information possible.

A related concern is that standards for the results of these question evaluation steps are not clear-cut. For example, it was suggested that questions that led respondents to ask for clarification in 15% of pretest interviews deserve to be flagged as problems. Empirically, it has been found that there usually is an identifiable problem with questions that generate that behavior that often. Nonetheless, it certainly is an arbitrary standard. Given that 100% standardized comprehension is not going to be achieved, what percentage of the population can seriously misunderstand a question before a researcher decides it is a problem?

These are not easy questions to answer, and they probably cannot be answered out of the context of the research objective. Some question misunderstandings will threaten the value of the data more than others. As researchers become more experienced with these evaluative techniques, and as they become better at quantifying the results from cognitive interviews and interviewer ratings, it seems likely that clearer standards may emerge.

Finally, it should be reiterated that the evaluation techniques described in this chapter focus on the process of data collection: how respondents understand and answer questions and how interviewers use questions. It is easy to demonstrate, and has been demonstrated, that the presence of the kinds of problems that will be identified in the evaluation strategies used in this chapter will produce error in survey data (e.g., Fowler, 1992; Fowler & Mangione, 1990; Mangione et al., 1992). Nonetheless, the fact that questions are consistently understood, can be answered, and are administered in a standardized way does not necessarily mean that the answers are accurate and valid measures of what the researcher is trying to measure. Further work is necessary in order to assess the validity of data emanating from survey questions. Strategies for doing those evaluations are the topic of the next chapter.

6

Assessing the
Validity of Survey Questions

The topic of this chapter is how to evaluate whether or not the answers to questions are valid measures of what researchers are trying to measure. In Chapter 5, the various steps to pretest questions all focused on the process of data collection: how questions were administered, how they were understood, and how they were answered. To the extent that data collection is not carried out well, the validity of survey measurement will likely be reduced. However, none of the steps in Chapter 5 provides a statistical assessment of the amount of error in answers to survey questions. That is the topic of this chapter.

There are four approaches to evaluating the validity of survey measures:

1. studies of patterns of association;
2. comparison of results from alternative forms of the same question;
3. comparing answers to survey questions with information derived from other sources, such as records; and
4. asking the same questions twice of the same respondents, and comparing results; or asking the same question of more than one person, then comparing the results. (Technically, these are measures of reliability, but unreliable questions also have low validity.)

STUDYING PATTERNS OF ASSOCIATION

When survey questions are designed to measure subjective phenomena, the evidence for how well measurement has occurred must be somewhat indirect. Because we cannot observe directly the subjective states of people, we must be content with inferences based on the premise that if we measured what we think we measured, it should behave in certain predictable ways (Turner & Martin, 1984; Ware, 1987). The foundation for the assessment of validity of this sort is called "construct validity" (Cronbach & Meehl, 1955).

There are three very closely related approaches to assessing such validity, essentially based on the same approach:

1. Construct validity
2. Predictive validity
3. Discriminant validity

Construct validity: if several questions are measuring the same or closely related things, then they should be highly correlated with one another.

Predictive validity: the extent to which a measure predicts the answers to some other question or a result to which it ought to be related.

Discriminant validity: the extent to which groups of respondents who are thought to differ in what is being measured, in fact, do differ in their answers.

Suppose we take an example of a measure of health status, how healthy people think they are.

Example 6.1: On a scale from zero to ten, where ten is the best health your health could be and zero is the worst your health could be, what number would you say best describes your health at the present time?

Suppose there were some other questions about health status that were asked in the survey such as:

Example 6.2: In general, how would you rate your health—excellent, very good, good, fair, or poor?

Example 6.3: Compared to other people your age, would you say your health is better, worse, or about the same?

Although each of these questions is worded differently, the underlying concept that the researchers were trying to measure is probably the same. One kind of evidence that the initial question, rating health from zero to ten, was a valid measure of health status is the extent to which it correlates with other measures that purport to measure health status.

An obvious caveat is that a test of validity is no better than the questions used to validate the measure. Hence, if two questions designed to measure health status do not correlate highly, that fact by itself does not tell us which question is a poor measure of health status. One or the other question, or both, can be a poor measure to yield that result. However, if there are several measures of health status, or closely related concepts, against which to test the answers to a question, researchers can build up a case for the likely validity of any particular question from the pattern of associations with other questions.

In addition, the researcher can go on to look at predictive validity. For example, we may hypothesize that poor health leads to use of medical services. Thus, on average over time, we would expect those who rated their health lower to have seen doctors more often, to be more likely to have been hospitalized, and perhaps to have missed more days of work because of illness. If we have information about those facts, we could see how well health status at a particular time predicted future utilization of health care or work days lost.

With such a test, we would expect the correlations to be lower than those noted above. People who think they are in good health use medical services to some extent, and some conditions that lead to medical care or hospitalization are acute conditions that do not have a lasting effect on people's perceptions of their health status. Nonetheless, most researchers would be disappointed if there were not a positive, significant relationship between a measure of health status and use of medical services. Again, if there is not a positive relationship it could be either because the measures are not good or because the theory is wrong (health status is a poor predictor of use of health services).

Finally, an example of a test of discriminant validity would be that patients diagnosed as having a significant health condition should, on average, rate their health lower than those who have no such condition. Thus researchers might identify a set of patients who had been diagnosed as having had a heart attack, a stroke, or diabetes. They could compare the distributions of ratings of health status between those with such conditions and those without. Again, the theory would be that those who know they have a serious health condition should, in fact, rate their health status lower than those who have no such conditions. To the extent that that is not true, it casts doubt on whether the answers to the question are measuring what researchers are trying to measure.

Studies such as these should routinely be done to evaluate the validity of subjective measures. Virtually any time a large-scale survey is done, there is the potential to do some evaluative studies such as those outlined above. One of the responsibilities of a survey researcher in the process of evaluating questions is to do those analyses that describe the extent to which answers to key subjective questions have predictable relationships.

VALIDATING AGAINST RECORDS

Individualized Record Checks

Although in theory it should be easier to validate the reporting of factual information than of subjective states, in reality it is not very easy to do. First, of course, a main reason people do surveys is to collect information that is not easily available from other sources. In particular, it is unusual to be able to do a cross-section sample survey, then to go back to some record source and evaluate the accuracy of reporting.

Most studies to evaluate the validity of reporting of factual data have been special-purpose studies specifically designed to assess the validity of the survey data. Cannell and associates have carried out several such studies. Patients were sampled from hospital discharge records. Then interviewers were sent to households in which known patients lived, and they carried out a standard health interview. The quality of reporting of hospital events were evaluated by comparing the survey reports with hospital records (Cannell, Fisher, & Bakker, 1965; Cannell & Fowler, 1965). Densen, Shapiro, and Balamuth (1963), Locander, Sudman, and Bradburn (1976), Loftus, Smith, Klinger, and Fiedler (1991), and Madow (1967) authored studies using similar designs.

In a parallel design, the reporting of crime victimization in surveys was evaluated by drawing samples from police records. Households in which known victims were thought to live were sampled, interviewers visited households to carry out a standard crime survey, and the accuracy of reporting of criminal events was evaluated by comparing the survey reports with the results from police records (Lehnen & Skogan, 1981).

Record-check studies are the best way to learn how well people report certain events and the characteristics of events that are reported inaccurately. For example, in the studies of hospitalization reporting done by Cannell, it was learned that hospital events that occurred more than ten months prior to the interview were distinctively likely to be unreported. It also was learned that very short hospital stays were underreported (Cannell, Marquis, & Laurent, 1977). From the crime surveys, it was found that respondents were not very good at reporting personal crimes (as contrasted with household crimes) that occurred to other family members over a one-year period.

As valuable as these studies have been, there also are limitations to what can be learned from such studies. The most important limitation is that only certain kinds of errors can be detected with such designs. If a sample is drawn from those known to have had an experience, such as being hospitalized or being a victim of a crime, the designs are excellent for detecting underreporting: failure to report an event that actually occurred. The designs also enable one to detect the accuracy with which details of events, such as the length of a hospital stay or the condition for which patients were treated in the hospital, are reported. However, such designs provide little opportunity for measuring overreporting: reporting an event as occurring within the time period when in fact there was no such event (Marquis, 1978). Finally, of course, records are imperfect; they contain error. Hence, estimates of survey errors based on record checks are themselves subject to error.

In addition, the kinds of reporting that can be checked with such designs may not be representative of all the events in which a researcher is interested. For example, in the National Crime Survey, researchers are interested in estimates of rates at which people are victimized. They ask for reports of experiences such as burglary, robbery, and car theft over the previous year. Most car thefts are reported to the police because of the insurance implications of car theft, but only a minority of robberies and attempted burglaries are reported to police. When a record-check study is based on a sample of events reported to the police, those events are not completely representative of all such crimes. The crimes reported to the police are distinctively likely to involve significant loss, or they may be events that have more impact for other reasons. A record-check study based only on events reported to police may overestimate how good the reporting would be for those similar events that did not find their way into police records. Thus a second limitation of such studies is the extent to which the events for which record checks can be done are actually representative of the universe in which researchers are interested (Lehnen & Skogan, 1981).

A third limit to such studies is that many of the most interesting and important things we ask people to report are virtually impossible to validate. For example, many surveys are aimed at measuring alcohol consumption or drug use. However, it is extraordinarily difficult to design a study that would provide an independent measurement of people's behavior in these respects. There have been studies that have tried. The use of marijuana can be detected in urine tests. Cigarette smoking can be measured in saliva and blood (e.g., Abrams, Follick, Biener, Carey, & Hitti, 1987; Benowitz, 1983). However, obviously these are very limited tests of what survey researchers ask in surveys. They want to ask about alcohol or marijuana consumption over a much longer period of time than an evening or a few days. The samples of people in such tests and the conditions under which they are interviewed also are likely to be very special and not very representative of typical surveys.

It is quite important to continue to do studies in which the quality of factual reporting is assessed against reliable outside data. Such studies are the basis for many of the important generalizations discussed in Chapter 2 about the nature of error in survey measurement and ways to reduce survey error. For example, one of the most important studies of the reporting of sensitive material was a record-check study done by Locander, Sudman, and Bradburn (1976). Samples were drawn from public records of such things as bankruptcies and drunken driving arrests. Samples were randomized to various approaches to collecting data, including self-administration, telephone interviews, and surveys using the random response technique described in Chapter 2. Even though the sample of people who had experienced one of these events was not representative, they were the sorts of people who have bankruptcies and drunken driving arrests to report. Hence, that was an excellent design for assessing the relative value of various approaches to collecting data about sensitive topics.

Nonetheless, there will be limits to these studies. There are only so many things that can actually be checked. We need other ways to evaluate the quality of the data.

Aggregate Comparisons

In some cases, it is possible to evaluate the quality of data collected by survey by comparing survey results against some other independent aggregate estimate for the same population. For example, when the National Health Interview Surveys are done, researchers can compare the estimate from the surveys about the number of hospitalizations in a year with the number of hospitalizations from aggregate hospital data (Cannell, Fisher, & Bakker, 1965). In a similar way, the quality of data regarding alcohol consumption can be evaluated by making estimates of the total amount of alcohol consumption from survey-based data and from alcohol industry sources about the amount of alcohol sold. The quality of data stemming from surveys asking about money wagered on racehorses at tracks can be compared with estimates from the racing industries (Kallick-Kaufmann, 1979).

Once again, there are limits to the questions that such methods can be used to evaluate. There are no good records of many behaviors about which we want to ask. Often it is difficult to create exactly comparable estimates from surveys and from records. A lack of consistency between the two kinds of estimates does not necessarily reflect the quality of survey reporting.

For example, there are record-based sources of data about the quantity of medical care delivered that can be compared with survey-based estimates. However, household surveys leave out the medical care delivered to those in nursing homes. Also, a sample of data collected at a point in time obviously omits all the people who have died in the preceding year. Hence, when estimates are aggregated for a year, the medical care and hospitalization use of all those who have died are excluded from the interview data. Because people who are about to die consume an extraordinary amount of medical care, this lack of comparability between the two samples has a big effect on the resulting estimates.

In contrast, virtually all the people who wager at horse tracks live in housing units. People who are about to die or people who live in nursing homes are not distinctively high users of race tracks; quite the opposite. Hence, a population survey can cover very well the population that bets at race tracks and, indeed, it turned out that a survey-based estimate of legal betting at horse tracks matched almost identically the known amount of money wagered legally at horse tracks (Kallick-Kaufmann, 1979).

Obviously, any time a comparison is made between a survey-based estimate and an estimate from some other source, questions need to be asked about the populations covered and also about the accuracy of both sources. For example, medical records have been used to evaluate the quality of survey reporting of health conditions. The findings have consistently been that they do not match very well. However, when the results are analyzed, it is clear that there are as many problems with medical records as measures of the presence of health conditions as there are with surveys (Cannell, Marquis, & Laurent, 1977; Jabine, 1987; Madow, 1967). Survey reports suffer because patients lack knowledge about the names of their health conditions. Moreover, household respondents distort the presence of conditions in various ways. On the other hand, physicians are inconsistent about writing down the presence of health conditions in medical records. Also, patients have many health conditions about which physicians do not even ask. Hence, there are some conditions for which medical records are probably a better source of information than survey interviews; there are other conditions, such as tinnitus, skin rashes, hemorrhoids, and pain in joints for which patient interviews are almost certainly a better source of information than physician records.

COMPARING ALTERNATIVE QUESTION FORMS

One important way to evaluate survey questions as measures is to ask essentially the same question in two different forms, then compare the results.

When measuring subjective phenomena, there are no right or wrong answers. However, by asking alternative forms of questions to comparable samples, researchers can find out which characteristics of questions affect the answers they obtain.

Rasinski (1989) reports a series of tests using this design.

Example 6.4a: To what extent do you think that we should do more for people whose incomes are too low to buy the things they need?

Example 6.4b: To what extent to you think we should do more for people who are on welfare?

Although one could argue easily that people who are on welfare are those who do not have enough money to buy the things they need, it turns out those are not the same questions at all. When comparable samples were asked those two questions, there was much less positive sentiment when the word "welfare" was used than when it was not. By asking these parallel questions, Rasinski documented that a question that includes the term "welfare" probably confounds two issues that cannot be disassociated: how people feel about supporting those who lack money plus how people feel about those who are on welfare.

Schuman and Presser (1981) have used this design to study many characteristics of questions. For example, they learned that when a "don't know" option is offered explicitly to people, respondents are much more likely to choose that answer than when it is not offered and respondents have to insist on using the answer themselves.

Schuman and Presser did numerous experiments asking parallel questions, with only slightly changed wording. Their studies enabled them to identify words or terms that changed the meanings of questions, as in the welfare example above, and other examples where meanings were not changed. For example, "surgically end a pregnancy" turned out to be equivalent to the word "abortion" in opinion questions, even though some might have thought in advance that abortion was a more loaded term.

Researchers have also used these designs to look at order effects. Sometimes questions affect the meaning of the questions that follow them, in other cases not. Again, split designs, where question order is varied, have been used to evaluate the extent to which preceding questions affect the stimulus, the actual meaning of a particular question.

The basic question addressed in studies of measures of subject phenomena is whether two questions are the same or different. If the distribution of responses is different, the questions constitute different stimuli. In fact, of course, they could still be equally valid measures as reflected in how well they correlate. However, lack of comparability means they are not interchangeable.

When questions are asked to measure objective states or events, there are right or wrong answers. When two parallel forms of questions do not yield the same results, it clearly implies error in at least one question as a measure.

When parallel forms of questions about facts are asked, ideally a researcher would like to have some basis for deciding which answers are best. If there is some way of checking the survey reports against a credible source, then direct evaluation is possible. However, in the usual situation where such validating checks are not possible, sometimes there are bases for choosing which distribution is likely to be best. For example, in studies of reporting of doctor visits, chronic conditions, and hospitalizations, Cannell and his associates frequently found underreporting to be the most significant problem. Hence, for many of his studies of alternative data collection procedures and designs of questions, Cannell used the criterion that questions that produced reporting of more such health events were likely to be better; that is, they were likely to contain less error (Cannell, Groves, Magilavy, Mathiowetz, & Miller, 1987; Cannell, Marquis, & Laurent, 1977; Cannell, Miller, & Oksenberg, 1981).

In a health study, pretests suggested that a question about exercise was producing underreporting because some respondents, though not all, were excluding walking for exercise from their answers. An alternative question was designed that explicitly told respondents that they could include walking. When it was tested, it was found that the percentage of people reporting that they exercised was considerably increased with the new version of the question. Based on the diagnosis of the problem with the original question and the way we designed the second question, it seemed that the evidence was clear that the second question was producing more valid data (Fowler, 1992).

As always, it is important to be cautious about interpreting the meaning of differences in the absence of corroborating data. More is not always better. An excellent example comes from research by Anderson, Silver, and Abramson (1988). Anderson was not evaluating question wording; she was evaluating the effects of interviewers on data. However, the principle is relevant here. In a political survey, she found that the black respondents were significantly more likely to report that they had voted in the last election to a black interviewer than to a white interviewer.

In the absence of other information, someone might have concluded that reporting to black interviewers was better. However, those who have been thinking about social desirability in answers will not be surprised to learn that the opposite was true. When voting behavior was checked against public records, it was found that the higher rate of reported voting was overreporting; the reporting to white interviewers was actually more accurate. When two estimates differ, it is always risky to infer which is best without a credible direct check on the quality of data. Concluding that one question is a better measure than another based solely on producing different results must be tentative at best.

CONSISTENCY AS A MEASURE OF VALIDITY

Usually, the consistency of answers over time is considered to be a measure of reliability. However, validity is limited by reliability. If answers are inconsistent, it necessarily implies invalidity as well (note that the converse is not true: consistent answers do not necessarily imply valid answers; Nunnally, 1978).

There are two main ways to measure consistency of survey answers:

1. The same person can be asked the same questions twice;
2. Two people can be asked the same question.

Obviously, inconsistency can be interpreted only as a sign of invalid reporting if we are sure the reality being described is the same.

Example: A respondent is asked about health insurance status during an interview; a reinterview is then conducted one week later during which, among other things, the respondent is again asked about health insurance. It is very unusual for health insurance to change in one week. Inconsistency in the answers would constitute compelling evidence of error in one or both answers. In fact, it would constitute a very conservative (low) estimate of error, because there are forces— including recall of the original answer—that would push respondents toward repeating the answers given during the initial interview.

Example: Two members of the same household are interviewed. Their interviews include common questions about household characteristics, such as household size, total family income, and health insurance coverage for themselves and other household members. Inconsistency in those answers would constitute evidence of error in the reporting of one or both respondents.

Other similar studies have been done to evaluate the quality of proxy reporting. In such studies, self-reporting is usually, but not always, assumed to be best when there is a difference between what people report about themselves and others report for them (Berk, Horgan, & Meysers, 1982; Clarridge & Massagli, 1989; Groves, 1989; Hauser & Massagli, 1983).

Consistency is clearly an important way to gain information about validity. Moreover, information about consistency is comparatively easy to collect. Reinterviews are a particularly straightforward, and underutilized, strategy to measure data quality. Although interpretation of results is sometimes problematic, such studies have a place in a total program of assessing the validity of answers to questions.

CONCLUSION

Readers no doubt will reach this point feeling that evaluating the validity of questions is not easy. That is a correct conclusion. Virtually every approach to evaluating the validity of questions discussed in this chapter is limited, either in the kinds of questions that can be evaluated or in the generalizability of the conclusions about validity that are reached. Nonetheless, it is important that researchers continue to evaluate the quality of reporting resulting from surveys whenever possible. Although imperfect, the results from such validating efforts provide critical evidence of the quality of survey data. They provide a stimulus to researchers to continue to work on improved measurement. They serve as important reminders to users of survey data about the appropriate uses and the limits to which survey measurement can be put.

Correlational studies, looking at the patterns of association of important variables, can almost always be done in the context of a survey analysis. Such evaluative analyses should be a routine part of any survey project. In addition, some of the special-purpose evaluations described in this chapter also can be built easily into many survey projects.

Parallel question designs, selective checks of surveys against existing records, and, particularly, aggregate estimates wherever they are possible, help to shed light on what the enterprise is about. Sometimes the results are ambiguous; however, almost always they stimulate learning and understanding, and those are important goals.

7

Question Design and
Evaluation Issues in Perspective

The quality of data from a survey depends on the size and representativeness of the sample from which data are collected, the techniques used for collecting data, the quality of interviewing, if interviewers are used, and the extent to which the questions are good measures. Methodologists have a concept that they call total survey design (Groves, 1989; Horvitz & Lessler, 1978). By that, they refer to the perspective of looking at all sources of error, not just a single source, when making survey design decisions. The quality of data from a survey is no better than the worst aspect of the methodology.

When Sudman and Bradburn (1974) looked at sources of error in surveys, they concluded that perhaps the major source of error in survey estimates was the design of survey questions. When Fowler and Mangione (1990) looked at strategies for reducing interviewer effects on data, they, too, concluded that question design was one of the most important roads to minimizing interviewer effects on data. Moreover, although the design of surveys often involves important trade-offs, improving the design and evaluation of survey questions is one of the least expensive components of the survey process. Compared with significantly increasing the size of a sample, or even the efforts required to improve response rates significantly, improving questions is very cost effective. Thus, from the perspective of total survey design, investing in the design and evaluation of questions is a best buy, one of the endeavors that is most likely to yield results in the form of better, more error-free data.

The book has covered many issues, some big, some small, that affect the quality of questions as measures. In this final chapter, we attempt to summarize the main points to provide some perspective on the most important issues to which to attend.

Factual Questions

Almost certainly, the biggest problem with questions designed to measure facts and objective events is the failure to make the step from the question objective to a set of questions that people can answer. Too often, questions are simply a repetition of the question objectives. The key principles are straightforward:

1. Ask people questions they can answer.
2. Make sure that all the key terms and concepts are clearly defined, so people know what question they are answering and they are all answering the same question.
3. Provide a context in which people will see answering questions accurately to be the best way to serve their own interests.

One further point should be made about interviewer-administered surveys. Attention must be paid to the fact that the survey instrument is also a protocol for an interaction. Attending to the sequence of questions and the way that answers to prior questions will affect the subsequent question-and-answer process can be a key part of improving the standardization of data collection and making the interview a positive data collection experience.

Measuring Subjective States

The primary problem for designers of measures of subjective states, like those of objective phenomena, is defining the objectives. A clear statement of what is to be measured is one key to the solution of many question design problems. Most often, the specification of measurement of objectives will take the form of wanting to place the respondent on a continuum or place the respondent's perceptions of something else on a continuum.

Once the objectives are specified in a clear way, the three key standards for subjective questions are that:

1. the terms of a question be clear, so everyone is answering the same question;
2. the response task is appropriate to the question and is relatively easy for most people to perform; and
3. the response alternatives are designed so that respondents who differ in fact in their answers will be distributed across the response alternatives.

In addition to these basic principles, it also is valuable to maximize the extent to which answers to questions provide measures for all respondents, not just a subset. Careful examination and pretesting of questions, to identify those that have hidden contingencies in order for them to be meaningful questions, can greatly improve the quality and efficiency of survey measurement. In the tradition of personality testing, when testers could include extraordinarily long inventories of questions, it may have been valuable to include items that provided useful information about small segments of respondents. However, respondent burden is a major concern in general-purpose surveys. Although multi-item measures can greatly improve the measurement process, particularly for subjective phenomena, investigators also have a responsibility to minimize respondent burden and to place people on continua as efficiently as possible. The information contained in the answers to 20- or 30-item scales can virtually always be reproduced with a small subset of those items, if they are carefully chosen. In this context, choosing items that provide the most information about each respondent is the efficient, and indeed ethical, way to proceed for measures of this sort.

Finally, having respondents place rated items, themselves or others, on scales, rather than using an agree-disagree format, will almost always provide better measurement both from the point of view of the simplicity of the task and the amount of information derived from each question.

Testing Questions

Focus groups, group discussions, cognitive interviews, and field pretests that include coding interviewer and respondent behavior should be a standard part of the development of any survey instrument.

The most important three premises for the evaluation of survey questions are:

1. Questions need to be consistently understood.
2. Questions need to pose tasks that people can perform.
3. Questions need to constitute an adequate protocol for a standardized interview, when interviewers are involved.

These goals seem so self-evidently valuable it is hard to believe that all survey questions do not meet these standards. However, they do not. In one study of 60 questions drawn from government and academic survey instruments, a clear majority were identified as failing to meet one or more of these basic criteria (Oksenberg, Cannell, & Kalton, 1991). On average, over a third of all survey questions are subject to significant interviewer effects on results (Groves, 1989), and there is clear evidence that questions that require probing and clarification by interviewers are most likely to be affected by interviewers (Mangione, Fowler, & Louis, 1992).

Cognitive interviews and behavior coding field pretests provide reliable, replicable information about question problems. The problems identified can be corrected, and the results are better data (e.g., Fowler, 1992; Oksenberg et al., 1991; Royston, 1989).

There is still work to be done to refine these procedures, to develop better and clearer standards for question problems, and to improve the generalizations about how to solve the problems that are identified with these processes, yet one of the important realities for students and researchers to grasp is that many of the worst question problems can be identified with simple, informal testing. Try questions on friends, parents, or children. Have them answer the test question, then describe in narrative form how they understood the question and how they arrived at the answer. Although rigorous, routine testing is necessary to advance survey science, better questions and better measurements result whenever researchers take steps to critically evaluate how consistently people can understand and answer their questions.

Evaluating the Validity of Questions

Around 1970, Robinson and associates published a critical evaluation of common survey measures of social psychological states and political attitudes (Robinson, Rusk, & Head, 1968; Robinson & Shaver, 1973). Those books were embarrassing testimony to how little attention was given to the assessment of how well commonly used questions performed as measures.

Twenty years later, progress has been made. A recent book by Robinson, Shaver, and Wrightsman (1991), which covers ground similar to the earlier volumes, finds many more standard measures that have been carefully evaluated. McDowell and Newell (1987) review common measures of health status and quality of life, again finding some encouraging trends with respect to the studies that have been done, particularly of more recently developed measures. A recent book by Stewart and Ware (1992) provides a kind of prototype for systematically developing measures of important health concepts.

Increasingly the word is out that particularly when scales and indices are used, validation studies are necessary. On occasions, measures are referred to as if being "validated" was some absolute state, such as beatification. Validity is the degree of correspondence between a measure and what is measured. Measures that can serve some purpose well are not necessarily good for other purposes. For example, some measurements that work well for group averages and to assess group effects are quite inadequate at an individual level (Ware, 1987). Validation studies for one population may not generalize to others. Kulka et al. (1989) report on a set of items to measure mental distress that differentiated extremely well between mental patients as a group and the general population. However, when those same items were used in a general population sample, they correlated very poorly at the individual level with independent clinical assessments of psychological problems.

The challenges at this point are of two sorts. First, we need to continue to encourage researchers routinely to evaluate the validity of their measurement procedures from a variety of perspectives. Second, we particularly need to develop clear standards for what validation means for particular analytic purposes.

Conclusion

To return to the topic of total survey design, no matter how big and representative the sample, no matter now much money is spent on data collection and what the response rate is, the quality of the resulting data from a survey will be no better than the questions that are asked. In 1951, Stanley Payne titled his landmark book, *The Art of Asking Questions*. We now know we can do better than that. Although we can certainly hope that the number and specificity of principles for good question design will grow with time, the principles outlined in this book constitute a good, systematic core of guidelines for writing good questions. In addition, although the development of evaluative procedures will also evolve with time, cognitive testing, good field pretests, and appropriate validating analyses provide scientific, replicable, and quantified standards by which the success of question design efforts can be measured. In short, at this point, there is no excuse for question design to be treated as an artistic endeavor. Rather, it should be treated as a science.

Unfortunately, there is a long history of researchers designing questions, in a haphazard way, that do not meet adequate standards. Moreover, we have a large body of social and medical science, collected over the last 50 years, that includes some very bad questions. The case for holding on to those questions that have been used in the past, in order to track change or to compare new results with those from old studies, is not without merit. However, a scientific enterprise is probably ill served by repeatedly using poor measures, no matter how rich their tradition. In the long run, science will be best served by using survey questions that have been carefully and systematically evaluated and that do meet the standards enunciated here. There is work to be done so that researchers routinely build in the kind of pretest and question evaluation procedures necessary to ensure that their questions are good. Such processes are increasingly being used, and it is to be hoped that this book will make a contribution to the further development and improvement of the question design and evaluation process.

Appendix A: Commonly Used Measurement Dimensions

In this section, we are going to critically evaluate some common approaches to asking questions about commonly measured subjective and objective phenomena.

1. Measuring frequency
2. Measuring quantity
3. Measuring feelings
4. Answering evaluative questions
5. Measuring satisfaction
6. Rating agreement
7. Measuring priorities
8. Dealing with people who "don't know"

Obviously, the very best question will depend on the research context and what the researcher is trying to do. One useful step is to look at how other researchers have measured these dimensions or addressed these issues. That is always good practice. However, the goal of Appendix A and Appendix B is to help readers think about, and choose among, the various alternative questions that could be used.

Measuring Frequency

Certainly asking people questions about the frequency with which they do various things is one of the most common tasks in survey research. Respondents are asked how frequently they consume alcohol, use marijuana, go to the bank, eat meat, go to the doctor, and have sexual relations.

Consider the following set of response categories:

More than once a day

Almost every day

A few times a week

About once a week

Two or three times a month

About once a month
Less than once a month
A few times a year
Once a year or less

The response categories in this scale cover a wide continuum. Which of the categories in the scale are appropriate depends, of course, on what is being asked. For things that a person might do frequently, such as eat or drink common foods, categories at the frequent end of the scale might be used. A different part of the scale would likely be appropriate for recreational activities such as going to the opera or going to a movie.

A fundamental problem with a question oriented toward this response task is the assumption of some kind of regularity. Although some sorts of behaviors lend themselves to regularity, irregularity is probably more common. Moreover, even for activities that are done regularly by some people, such as going to church or drinking alcohol, there are other people whose patterns are more erratic.

Generally speaking, measures of frequency are done better by asking people to estimate the number of times they have actually done something in an appropriate period of time. The period of time will vary depending on what behavior is being measured.

Example A.1: In the last 14 days, on about how many different days did you have any wine, beer, or liquor to drink at all?

Example A.2: In the last 30 days, on about how many different days would you say that you did physical exercise for a period of at least 20 minutes?

Example A.3: In the past 12 months, how many different times were you admitted to a hospital as a patient overnight or longer?

The most important criticism of questions that cover a short time span, such as a week or two, is that the time period may not be representative. Hence, if the past two weeks have been atypical, the person may not be characterized well as, for example, a heavy or a light drinker. On the other hand, asking people to report frequency of behaviors, even if they have to be estimates, solves the problem of trying to impose some kind of regularity or pattern on people's behaviors.

Another approach to frequency might be something like the following:

Very often	Often
Fairly often	Sometimes
Occasionally	Rarely
Rarely	Never
Never	

Response scales such as the above are somewhat more difficult to interpret than responses that use numbers. A great advantage of asking people to report frequencies over some period of time is that it avoids the problem of different definitions of what constitutes "often." Respondents who differ in their conception of what constitutes "often" may give different answers for that reason rather than because of their differing behaviors. However, if a question is being asked that seems to defy quantification, and the general purpose is to sort people into very broad categories, a question like the above might work fine.

Frequency is particularly difficult to ask about when the question includes two things that could vary. For example, if one wanted to know about popcorn eating at the movies, the absolute frequency would be the product of the number of times a person went to the movies multiplied by the percentage of times the popcorn was purchased. For such questions, a proportional sort of question might be best such as:

Always	Almost always	Always
Usually	More than half the time	Usually
A good bit of the time	About half the time	Sometimes
Some of the time	Less than half the time	Rarely
Rarely	Rarely	Never
Never	Never	

The above three scales are all approaches to measuring something as a proportion of time or events. They also might be the right way to quantify feelings such as pain or fatigue. Talking in terms of the proportion of time that a person was in pain or felt fatigue might be a better way to ask the question than asking about the number of days on which fatigue was felt. In the same way, if a student was asked how frequently homework papers were produced on time, proportion might be the right way to ask the question.

Several differences among the response tasks above are worth noting.

1. People taking scholastic aptitude tests are taught seldom to answer "always" or "never." For some questions, "always" or "never" are in fact reasonable answers that researchers want to identify. "Always" using birth control is importantly different from "almost always." "Never" fainting is importantly different from "rarely."

2. The scale that uses proportion of time, such as more than half the time or less than half the time, may be somewhat less subject to individual variability in interpretation of adjectives than the other scales. Scales that are quantifiable, as compared with those that rely purely on adjectives, also have some advantages in translations across languages.

3. Scales of frequency pose some difficulty in defining the middle or intermediate categories. "Usually" or "always" on the positive end and "rarely" or "never" on the negative end are fairly well defined and commonly

understood. Terms like "some of the time," "a good bit of the time," "sometimes," and "fairly often" are harder terms to work with in the middle of a continuum of frequency. The scales above probably do a fairly good job of dealing with that problem, but it is a continuing challenge for survey researchers to do a good job of labeling spots on a frequency continuum in and around the middle of the scale.

Measuring Quantity

Many survey questions also try to measure quantity or size. Typical examples are "How much of a problem do you have?" "To what extent are you affected by something?" or "How much do you care?" Two common approaches to labeling a continuum of quantity include:

A lot/a great deal	Big
Some	Medium
Only a little	Small
Not at all	None at all

It turns out that it is difficult to break the continuum of quantity into many more than four categories using adjectives. One could add "very small problem" between "small" and "none." One could add "almost not at all." However, four or five adjectives is about all that can be sustained.

Subjective sense of quantity is a measure that lends itself to a numerical scale.

Example A.4: Think of the scale from 0 to 10, where numbers 8, 9 and 10 stand for a very great amount; numbers 0, 1 and 2 stand for none or a little; and the numbers in the middle, 3 through 7, are somewhere in the middle. What number would you assign to the amount of pain you have been experiencing over the last month?

Measuring Feelings

Rating how respondents feel about things, from positive to negative, is another of the most common survey tasks that people are given. A common scale for measuring feeling is:

Very positive

Generally positive

Mixed: About equally positive and negative

Generally negative

Very negative

Here are some faces expressing various feelings. Below each is a letter.

   A   B   C   D   E   F   G

Which face comes closest to expressing how you feel about _____?

Figure A.1. Using Faces to Measure Feelings
SOURCE: Andrews and Withey (1976). Reprinted with permission.

WARM   100   _____   Very warm or favorable feeling
           85   _____   Good warm or favorable feeling
           70   _____   Fairly warm or favorable feeling
           60   _____   A bit more warm or favorable than cold feeling
           50   _____   No feeling at all
           40   _____   A bit more cold or unfavorable feeling
           30   _____   Fairly cold or unfavorable feeling
           15   _____   Quite cold or unfavorable feeling
COLD   0   _____   Very cold or unfavorable feeling

Where would you put _____ on the feeling thermometer?

Figure A.2. Using the Feeling Thermometer to Measure Feelings
SOURCE: Andrews and Withey (1976). Reprinted with permission.

Another approach is the "Delighted to Terrible" scale:

Delighted
Pleased
Mostly satisfied
Mixed
Mostly dissatisfied
Unhappy
Terrible

Two other approaches that use visual aids are presented in Figures A.1 and A.2.

All of the above have been used in numerous surveys. Andrews and Withey (1976) did a systematic evaluation of different ways of measuring how people felt. Their conclusion was that the Delighted to Terrible scale was the best in terms of its general utility and other psychometric properties, such as how well it spread people and the results of construct validity assessments. However, the faces and the 10-point thermometer proved to work almost as well. One great advantage of both of the latter scales is that they do not depend on adjectives. Hence, although the strength of the Delighted to Terrible scale may be the effective way in which the scale points are communicated consistently to people by way of language, a weakness is the difficulty in translating that across languages. The Delighted to Terrible scale is very long for use on the telephone, whereas the faces and thermometer require respondents to be exposed to visual stimuli. Of course, a numerical scale, such as 0 to 10, without visual aids, can be used to measure feelings just as it can be used to measure quantity.

One final note is in order about using numerical scales for measuring feelings. Although every point on a continuum does not need to be defined, it probably is important to define a midpoint, the place where positive feelings turn into negative feelings. That can be done adjectivally, as it is done on the Feeling Thermometer above. Another way of doing it is to give people a numerical task of rating their feelings from −5 to +5, with 0, obviously, being the midpoint, when positive feelings turn to negative.

Asking Evaluative Questions

The feeling questions outlined above are for use when people are asked to rate how they feel about things. The questions in this section are for use when people are asked to say how they evaluate something. The two may be correlated, but they are not identical.

The most commonly used evaluative scale may be:

Excellent
Very good
Good
Fair
Poor

An almost equally common rating scale is 0-10, where 10 is as good as it can be and 0 is as bad as it can be. The excellent-to-poor scale is a very easy one to use. Because people are familiar with the words, it is not difficult to remember. The disadvantage is that it has only five categories, and for many ratings it turns out that people tend toward the positive end of the scale. Therefore, it may be valuable to use rating scales that have more points. It is hard to think of adjectives to add to the continuum between good and excellent that have meaning and do not sound redundant. For that reason, the numerical scale approach from 0 to 10 may in fact be a preferred solution for many rating tasks.

Measuring Satisfaction

Measuring satisfaction is conceptually different from measuring evaluation, though they often would be judged to be highly related. Theoretically, satisfaction is the relationship between what people want and what they get.

Very satisfied	Completely satisfied	Perfectly satisfied
Generally satisfied	Mostly satisfied	Slightly dissatisfied
Somewhat dissatisfied	Mixed—equally satisfied	Somewhat dissatisfied
Very dissatisfied	and dissatisfied	Very dissatisfied
	Mostly dissatisfied	
	Completely dissatisfied	

One question people would raise about the first scale is the fact that the words are not symmetrical. However, one problem with satisfaction as a label is that "somewhat satisfied" may be negative. "Generally satisfied" is almost certainly a more positive state than "somewhat satisfied," and the first scale is probably more symmetrical (cognitively, if not verbally) than if "somewhat satisfied" was the second category.

It also should be noted that there is no reason why the adjectives along a continuum that go through zero need to be exactly the same on each side of a midpoint. The goal is to find adjectives that consistently communicate different spots on a continuum. The characterization of satisfaction may be one for which this is best done by using somewhat different words on the opposite sides of the midpoint.

Whether or not a midpoint is necessary is another issue. Conceptually, the notion of balancing satisfaction and dissatisfaction may be wrong for some tasks. Satisfaction is really about what people get. Being less than completely satisfied and not getting exactly what a person wants are deviations from perfection. There is a good case to be made that we are simply scaling degrees of dissatisfaction as we move further away from "completely satisfied." That orientation leads to the righthand column of responses.

Finally, researchers should be careful to consider the possibility that respondents do not care about some aspect of their life. A satisfaction question should be asked only about things with which respondents come in contact and for which they have some kind of expectations. For example, if a person walks to work, a rating of satisfaction with available parking may be meaningless. If it is not reasonable to think that all respondents have expectations about something, it might be better to have them do a rating task than to have them report on their satisfaction.

Rating Agreement

Completely agree	Strongly agree	Completely true
Generally agree	Agree	Somewhat true
Generally disagree	Disagree	Somewhat untrue
Completely disagree	Strongly disagree	Completely untrue

There is a discussion in Chapter 3 about the conceptual complexity of combining "strength" of feelings and agreement in a single scale. Although the middle form of the scale above may be the most commonly used, there is good reason to avoid that particular approach. Either of the other two scales, which focus on the cognitive aspects of the task, are more likely to prove satisfactory measures.

Whether one prefers the "true" formulation of the response task or the "agreement" formulation of the response task depends on whether it is an evaluative task or a cognitive task. If the question is how close preferences come to matching a statement, then asking about the agreement makes more sense. If the question is how close perceptions come to a particular statement, then the correct dimension is perception of truthfulness.

We should reiterate two cautions expressed in the parallel section in Chapter 3. In theory, there is a middle point, where a person is perfectly ambivalent about whether to agree or disagree. Many researchers offer a middle category (undecided, neither agree nor disagree). A category like that will appeal to some respondents, but it probably does not hurt to make respondents commit themselves. Moreover, that middle category becomes a haven for those people who lack the information needed to have an opinion about a question. Those people are different from ambivalent informed people. They should be identified separately, with a screening question, and they should not be placed in a middle category between those who agree and those who disagree.

Measuring Priorities: Rank Order Versus Ratings

Researchers often want to measure priorities, and one obvious approach is to ask people to rank order some alternatives:

Example A.5: Here is a list of problems some people are concerned about. Which of these do you consider most important?

a. Reducing crime in the streets.

b. Reducing air pollution.

c. Providing jobs for those who need them.

d. Providing health care to those who need it.

e. Lowering federal income taxes.

Respondents could be asked sequentially for the most important, next most important, etc. If the survey is done in person or with a self-administered form, they could rank order the items from 1 to 5.

Example A.6: Consider a scale from 0 to 10, where 8, 9, and 10 are the highest priority; 0, 1, and 2 are low priority; and 3 through 7 are in between. What number would you give to the priority of (EACH).

The second kind of task is easier for respondents, particularly on the telephone. By definition, the rank order task does not give us information about how much people care about any item. In theory, a respondent could consider even the top-rated item as unimportant or the lowest rated item as very important. The data from the rating task can produce ties; all the items could be rated 10. However, the average across groups of respondents usually will produce an ordering, if that is important, and in general, the multiple-rating task provides more information with less respondent effort. For most surveys, it probably represents a better approach.

Dealing With People Who "Don't Know"

There are many questions asked in surveys for which a "don't know" answer is not a plausible answer. Often, when respondents say "don't know," it is a response style that means that they have not thought very much about a topic, or they are not certain, among several response possibilities, which answer fits best. In such situations, researchers would probably prefer that the respondent work a little harder and come up with an answer.

When respondents are asked for their feelings, opinions, or evaluations of things outside themselves—public policies, political figures, institutions—it becomes quite plausible to think that they lack information in sufficient detail to provide a rating or have an opinion. When it is reasonable that a person might not actually know enough to answer a question, researchers would be best served if they developed an explicit strategy for screening out such people.

There are two ways to do this. First, there can be a screening question asked in advance of the opinion question.

Example A.7: The next question is about the Agricultural Trade Act of 1978. Do you feel familiar enough with that act to have an opinion about it or not?

Alternative Example A.7a: Thinking back to the terms of the Agricultural Trade Act of 1978, would you say that in general you were in favor of that act, opposed to that act, or are you not familiar enough with the act to have an opinion on that?

Either one of those approaches to screening respondents has two real advantages over ignoring the "don't know" possibility. First, it explicitly condones the notion that some people may not have enough information to answer a question, making it easier for respondents to admit to ignorance. More important, it defines a specific process for having respondents themselves decide whether or not they know enough to answer the question. In the absence of an explicit effort to identify people who are not familiar enough with a topic to answer a question, it turns out that interviewers and respondents are inconsistent in the way that they handle the uncertainty about whether a respondent should try to answer a question (e.g., Groves, 1989). Providing an explicit process improves the standardization of the measurement process.

> *Example A.8:* The next question is going to ask you about your opinions about the schools here in your town. Do you feel you have enough information about the schools to have an opinion about them?

A disadvantage of this explicit kind of screening question, as compared with building the "no opinion" alternative into the question, is that the respondent does not know what sorts of questions are going to be asked. It is easy to think of a respondent who would have opinions about some aspects of schools, but who would answer "no" to the above screening question. (Schwartz & Hippler, 1991). Although the general screening question about the Agricultural Trade Act may in fact have been a reasonable way to screen respondents, for many purposes the inclusion of a "no opinion" alternative among a set of response options may permit respondents to make a more informed judgment about whether or not they are able to answer questions. The downside of explicitly giving a "don't know" option is that the number of such answers will be increased. That is the reason why prior analysis of the nature of the response task is so important. If respondents are being asked about their firsthand experiences or feelings, minimizing unanswered questions, "don't knows" and others, is reasonable. On the other hand, when respondents are asked for the opinions or perceptions of things beyond their direct experience, a "don't know" response is a potentially meaningful answer, not missing data, and it is best obtained in an explicit, standardized way.

CONCLUSION

It always makes sense for people designing survey instruments to look at the way that other experienced researchers have designed survey questions. Two of the major resources in the United States are the General Social Survey, conducted by the National Opinion Research Center, and the surveys that are maintained by the Political Consortium at the University of Michigan.

In addition, regardless of how many times a question has been used, or by whom, survey questions need to be evaluated. They need to be evaluated carefully before a survey is launched, and the results also need to be evaluated from the perspective of the validity of the measurement that resulted. (See Chapters 5 and 6.)

Appendix B:
Measures of Common Covariates

In most surveys, researchers collect descriptive information about respondents against which to tabulate answers. Some of the most common such variables are:

1. age
2. gender
3. marital status
4. employment status
5. socioeconomic status (education, income, occupation)
6. religious preference or affiliation
7. race and ethnic background

In this appendix, we discuss alternative ways of asking questions about these respondent characteristics. Once again, the goal is not to prescribe the right questions for all surveys, but rather to raise some issues about how best to measure these that researchers may want to consider.

Age

The most obvious way to ask this question, probably, is:

Example B.1: How old are you?

Example B.1a: What is your age?

Comment: One possible ambiguity about these questions has to do with rounding. Some people may report how old they will be on the nearest birthday. An alternative wording that is common is:

Example B.1b: How old were you on your last birthday?

People do a fair amount of rounding when asked for their age. There is heaping at round numbers, such as numbers ending in 5 and 10. This suggests that some people prefer to give an approximate figure for their age, rather than giving an exact number. This may lead researchers to prefer asking a different question:

Example B.1c: In what year were you born?

When that question is asked, obviously the researcher has to do the calculation of age. "What was your date of birth?" is the question needed to calculate an exact age.

Finally, there clearly are respondents who are sensitive about their age and who would prefer to answer a question in general categories. If a researcher is only interested in analyzing respondents by large categories, they should be asked the question in that form.

Example B.1d: In which of these groups is your age: under 30, 30 to 44, 45 to 64, 65 or older?

Gender

This might be one of the most straightforward questions in survey research. The categories are clear and mutually exclusive. Almost all respondents have a clear notion of the answer.

Example B.2: Are you male or female?

This particular form of the question avoids interactions with the age of the respondent that man, woman, boy, and girl entail. Just about the only problem with this question is that interviewers are reluctant to ask it when they think it should be obvious, but it is not. In face-to-face interviews, this information usually is collected by interviewer observation, rather than by asking the question. On the telephone, however, although most often interviewers think they know the gender of their respondent, occasionally they are not certain. The wording above is as good as any.

Marital Status

Example B.3: Are you married, divorced, widowed, separated, or have you never been married?

This is one of several questions we will discuss that seems quite straightforward but in fact poses a number of potentially important problems.

One problem is the variation in the way that people go about dissolving or ending their marriages. Some people get a divorce, some people get a legal separation, and some people simply split up for a while. Alternatively, some married couples, people who consider themselves successfully married, live apart temporarily but would not consider themselves to be "separated."

The term "never married" is a better one than "single," which occasionally is seen in these questions. To many respondents, "single" simply means unmarried, which obviously can apply to several of the above categories.

Certainly the most troublesome status for some researchers is designated as "living as married." Some survey researchers have responded to the fact that some people live together, behaving in various ways similar to those who are married, but yet are not formally married, by adding this response alternative. Adding such a category to the list of acceptable "marital states" solves a problem about how to classify such people, and some respondents like having a category that seems to capture their situation so well. On the other hand, that category raises problems of definition. Whether researchers have actually gained useful information about respondent status by having that category is debatable.

The complexity comes from the fact that being married has various implications, depending on the analysis. For studies related to economic well-being, being married means that incomes and expenses are likely to be shared. For studies related to children, married parents mean potentially sharing child care and also having long-term economic responsibilities for support of children. For studies of social well-being, being married implies having a friend. For studies of risk of AIDS, being married suggests monogamy. It is not at all clear which of these, if any, is implied by choosing the category, "living as married."

The simple question with which this section started is carrying a great deal of weight, because it has embedded in it at least half a dozen questions. For many research purposes, four questions supply all the information needed, and in a better and more reliable form than the single summary question.

Example B.4: Are you married or unmarried now?

Example B.4a: (IF MARRIED) Are you and your (SPOUSE) living together now or living separately?

Comment: For many purposes, that is all the information that is needed. A bit of refinement might be gathered by adding a third question:

Example B.4b: (IF SEPARATELY) Do you consider the arrangement of living separately to be a temporary or a permanent arrangement?

In some cases, it also is useful to find out more about those who are not currently married. There are two main questions that one would like to ask in order to replicate the information that presumably we were getting in the initial question.

Example B.5: (IF NOT NOW MARRIED) Have you ever been married?

Example B.5a: (IF EVER MARRIED) Are you widowed, legally divorced, legally separated, or just living apart from your (SPOUSE)?

Comment: Notice that the people who said they were married and living separately would be classified with those who said they were not married, but had not legally separated.

Depending on the goals of the research, researchers might want to ask additional questions about the relationship between the respondent and previous spouses. In addition, if there are concerns such as sources of financial support or the availability of companionship for the respondent, those questions should be asked more directly, not inferred from the answer to a summary question about marriage.

Employment Status

The situation with employment status is very much the same as marital status.

Example B.6: Are you employed, on layoff from a job, unemployed, keeping house, a student, or retired?

In the 1950s, this may have been a reasonable question. Today, it is a very poor question. Among its problems, it violates two of the most important standards for a good survey question: the categories are neither well defined nor mutually exclusive.

Let us begin with the problems of overlapping categories. It is very common for people enrolled in educational programs also to be employed; the majority of students work to some extent, and a good number of people with full-time jobs are taking courses and seeking degrees.

The status of retired also is not clear. For many jobs—jobs in public safety and the armed forces stand out—it is possible to retire at a comparatively early age, far before the traditional 65. Such people often go on and take additional jobs. Are they retired, because they are on a retirement income from a long-time career, even though they are currently employed?

It also is becoming increasingly ambiguous as to what constitutes employment. A large number of people now work for pay but are not considered real employees; they do not receive benefits and the work could stop with a minimum of notice. If the goal is to find out if a person has any income as a result of work, such jobs certainly constitute employment. However, if the goal is to identify people who have a stable relationship with some kind of organization, the coding is more complex.

Once again, the basic problem is that about five or six questions are being asked at once. The question is asking respondents to do a complex coding task, rather than providing respondents with a set of questions that can be directly answered that will provide information the researcher needs to do the coding. The researchers' task, in this case, is to break down and identify exactly what kind of information is needed from an analytic perspective, then ask respondents to provide it. One possible series might look like the following. The usual first goal is to find out whether or not a person is working for pay. The question might be as simple as this:

Example B.7: Last week, did you receive any pay from a job or for work that you did?

Comment: Even this question is probably imperfect. For example, there are people who perform services who may not exactly consider it to be work. However, those issues are problems for a small segment of the population. People who have trouble with that distinction are certainly going to have more trouble with our initial summary question.

There undoubtedly are many other things researchers might want to know about the working situation. Does the person have one job or two jobs? Does the person work full-time or part-time? Is the person paid a salary or by the hour? Does the job have benefits, such as paid vacations and health insurance? How long has the person worked at the job? How secure does the person feel that the job can continue indefinitely?

These are all reasonable questions. Which of these are important depends on the research objectives. The answers to none of these questions can be directly inferred from the fact that a person chose "employed" as compared with some alternatives. If the researcher wants to know about these aspects of employment, questions must be asked.

If the person did not receive money in the past week, we might want to find out why. Several of the categories in the initial question have to do with classifying nonworking status. One critical concept is whether or not the status of "not working" is voluntary or involuntary. The question that the Bureau of Labor Statistics has relied on for many years to define involuntary unemployment is, "Have you been looking for work in the last four weeks?" Others have pointed out that this question is fraught with ambiguity, the key ambiguity being what constitutes "looking for work." It has been noted that people who have given up looking for work, and give a "no" answer to that question, become reclassified as voluntarily unemployed people. As usual, one bit of advice is to ask a more direct question. If the goal is to find out whether or not unemployment is voluntary, why not ask something like:

Example B.8: Would you say you are not working now mainly because you do not want to work right now, or mainly because you cannot find a job?

Asking questions about whether people are students should be a discrete line of inquiry.

Example B.9: During the past six months, have you taken any courses for credit toward a degree or diploma?

The advantage of this question is that it does not make assumptions about the pattern by which people acquire their educations. This particular question rules out adult education courses and technical training that is not part of a degree program. Obviously, one could ask other questions aimed at such activities. In addition, one could ask follow-up questions to find out what sort of degree the person was pursuing, whether enrollment was full-time or part-time, and so forth.

Finally, with respect to retirement, the main significance of that classification may be that it identifies a person who has decided not to do any more work for pay. For many purposes, simply the fact that the person is voluntarily out of the labor force is all that is needed. If a researcher is interested in future work plans, then a specific question is needed to identify those people who, at the moment, have no future plans to re-enter the labor force. The same applies to people who consider themselves temporarily or permanently out of the labor force because of disability.

Socioeconomic Status

Measures that researchers use as indicators of socioeconomic status include:

1. income
2. educational attainment
3. occupation

There generally are three different kinds of variables that people are actually trying to measure:

1. information or knowledge, along with some possibly related attitudes, that some people think go along with higher socioeconomic attainment
2. resources
3. social status or prestige

Occupation (or more generally, occupational status), income, and education all tend to be somewhat intercorrelated in a positive way. However, each has limitations, often very severe limitations, for capturing what researchers are truly after.

Educational attainment is probably the most generally useful and interpretable measure of the three. Simply knowing how many years of schooling a person has is only a rough indicator of knowledge, values, and training. Moreover, there have been trends over the years toward higher average levels of formal education, creating an interaction between age and educational attainment. Nonetheless, there is a reasonably straightforward basis for postulating a direct relationship between education and information. Moreover, educational attainment is not dependent on the circumstances of the respondent in a way that distorts the meaning of education, as is the case with income.

Income would seem likely to be the best, most direct measure of resources or financial well-being. However, that statement must be tempered by three complexities:

1. A person's resources may include not only current personal income but also the combined incomes of other family members.
2. Well-being is also affected by the availability of assets. That complexity particularly confuses comparing the well-being of young people, who typically have few assets other than income, with retirees, who are likely to have more assets.
3. Well-being is dependent not only on income but also on financial obligations. Given the same income, a single, unmarried person or retired person will be better off than someone responsible for providing for a family of four.

Obviously, if one is studying financial well-being in detail, one would want to collect information about all of these topics: income of other family members, assets, and financial responsibilities. However, the point is that knowing an individual's current income alone, without factoring in some of these other considerations, probably is quite an imperfect measure of financial well-being or resources.

Occupation, that is, the kind of job that a person occupies, is an even more complicated and probably less useful way of learning something about socioeconomic status. The notion of using occupation, usually of the "head of the family," as a measure of the social standing of that family has its roots in sociological theory, probably fairly traced to Karl Marx, who thought that the position of a person with respect to work defined his or her position in society. In survey research, a common strategy for making sense of the hundreds of different occupational classifications currently in use is to collapse them into eight or ten categories: professional, managerial, sales, clerical, skilled worker, semiskilled worker, service worker, and unskilled labor (plus farm owners and farm workers). These groupings were thought to roughly define an ordered set of occupational categories. The imperfection of the classification, however, is reflected in the fact that the "professional" category includes grade-school teachers, putting them in the top category, whereas "service workers" includes domestic helpers, people who work at McDonald's, and police officers and firefighters. The last two are often paid more than grade school teachers.

The meaning of occupation as a measure of social standing is also confused by the fact that in most two-adult households, there are two workers with two occupations.

A final barrier to routine use of occupation as a generally useful characteristic of respondents is the difficulty of the classification process itself. In order to code occupation, at least three questions are needed:

Example B.10: What kind of work do you do on your job?

Example B.10a: In what kind of business or organization do you work?

Example B.10b: Do you work for yourself or someone else?

Given the answers to these questions, quite a complex coding process must be applied, one that requires good training and supervision in order to carry it out in a reliable way.

When one is doing studies focused on workforce participation, having good information about occupations and the kind of work people do is essential. However, as a general descriptive characteristic of people, to be used as a covariate in analyzing their other answers, measuring current or past occupations is probably a poor choice for most surveys.

For most surveys, the most generally useful question to ask is:

Example B.11: What is the highest grade or year of school you have completed?

In all probability, asking income is done much more frequently than it needs to be. Moreover, for most of the analytic purposes for which it will be used, getting people's incomes in very broad categories is probably all that is required. The most usual, legitimate objective in measuring income is assessing something about the resources available to people. For that purpose, probably total family income for the preceding year is the best single measure.

Example B.12: We would like a general estimate of the total family income for you and for all family members living with you during (LAST YEAR). Considering income from all sources—from jobs, interest, rents, and so forth—for you and all family members living with you, what would you say was your total family income in 19__ before taxes—less than $20,000, $20,000 to $39,000, $40,000 to $59,000, or $60,000 or more?

It is quite obvious that this question, even in this simplified form, is very complicated and does not meet the standards articulated in this book very well. The reporting of income, if a good number is really required, will be improved if incomes from the various possible sources are asked about individually before the respondent is asked to give a total figure. Ask specific questions about pay for the respondent, pay for the respondent's family members, rents, welfare payments (if appropriate), Social Security, pensions, and interest. Then ask for a total. The number and complexity of categories can be elaborated, and for some purposes that is an important and useful thing to do.

Religion

Example B.13: Do you consider yourself to be Protestant, Catholic, Jewish, or some other religion, or do you have no preference?

A person's religion can be measured in one of three main ways:

a. the religious culture in which the person was raised;
b. the person's current self-perception; or
c. the person's affiliation with organized religion.

The three are interrelated: Adults are more likely than not to think of themselves in terms of the religions in which they were raised, and they are more likely than not to belong to religious groups that reflect their self-perceptions. However, there are some differences that result from the choice of one of these approaches.

The most important limitation of asking for membership as a way of classifying people religiously is that many people do not belong to organized religious groups. Membership varies by life cycle; young adults before marriage are less likely to have formal religious ties than people who are married and have children. In addition, formal religious affiliation varies by religious group; it is particularly significant that some groups require members to pay dues or membership fees in order to be formal members, whereas that is not true of others. Most important, because many people who have religious identities and beliefs do not belong to congregations, if affiliation is the measure of religious orientation, many people will not be classified at all.

Whether people should be classified religiously by how they were raised or by their current preference may depend on the purposes for which data are being collected. There are two advantages of asking people the religion in which they were raised. Some people can be put in a religious category on that basis who currently express no religious preference. Also, some people would argue that the important elements of religious orientation are developed during childhood. The disadvantage is that such a classification misses the changes from childhood to adulthood, including conversions, withdrawal from religious convictions that occurs in adulthood, or the development of new religious convictions and commitments that were not apparent during childhood.

Finally, the basic question at the beginning of this section used the term "Protestant," which is not a universally understood term. Some people who are Baptists or Methodists identify themselves that way, but not as Protestants. Moreover, there is not general agreement on exactly who constitutes a Protestant. For example, some people think any Christians who are not Roman Catholics are Protestants, whereas others have more refined definitions. Although the initial, basic question is imperfect, it probably is the most generally useful question to ask as a starter. As a follow-up, because the views and ideologies of Protestant sects vary greatly in the United States, it usually would be a good idea to ask a follow-up question: Is there any particular branch or denomination that you prefer?

Race and Ethnic Background

Race and ethnic background are, of course, not the same, though they are related at some level. The racial categories commonly used in the United States are:

Black
White
Asian (or Pacific Islander)
Native American Indian (Eskimo or Aleut)

Ethnic background sometimes refers to country of origin, such as Irish or Italian. However, culture and political systems do not always coincide. There are many countries that are considered Hispanic. Armenians and Jews are both ethnic and religious groups, and they "originate" from places other than Armenia (which was part of the U.S.S.R. until its demise) and Israel. Moreover, countries change. The political units in Eastern Europe and Africa were far different in 1993 from what they were in 1970. Thus identifying a person's ethnic or cultural heritage by country of origin can be elusive.

In the United States, the race "Asian" tends to be treated synonymously with being from an Asian country. However, of course, black and African American are not always the same.

Finally, language is another aspect of culture and background on which some researchers base questions.

Example B.14: Are you of Spanish or Hispanic origin?

Example B.14a: (IF YES) What group—for example, Mexican, Mexican American, Puerto Rican, Cuban, etc.

NOTE: Some people prefer the term "Native American" to "American Indian." However, in general surveys, people routinely interpret "Native American" to mean they were born in the United States. The term "Indian" is needed to make the meaning clear.

Example B.15: What is your race—American Indian, Asian, Black, White, or something else?

Example B.15a: (IF ASIAN) What group, for example, Chinese, Asian Indian, Hawaiian, Vietnamese, etc.?

This is a slight variation of the series of questions asked in the United States Census and in many government surveys. Culture, race, and country of origin are thoroughly mixed and confused in this series, reflecting a general confusion about what background characteristics matter.

Identifying Hispanics is routine in government surveys. Because what constitutes a Hispanic origin is not well defined, asking for "group," in a question that really is aimed at country of origin, is added as a check for respondents who are from places where Spanish is spoken who do not identify themselves as Hispanic, and to sort Hispanic people into subgroups. Asking about Hispanic origin before asking race is a good idea, because many Hispanics seem to resist racial classification until they have identified themselves as Hispanic (Martin, DeMaio, & Campanelli, 1990).

For many purposes, the single most useful question to ask adults, in combination with race, is "In what country were you born?" The impact of a foreign culture is greatest for those born outside the United States. Adults born in the United States were raised speaking English. For those who were foreign born, country of origin is an easy question to answer and provides considerable information about the respondent. It then permits the researcher to group countries in any way desired, rather than asking the respondents to classify themselves.

If cultural heritage is of great interest, the birthplace of the mother and father might be the next most useful information.

Example B.16: In what country was your (mother/father) born?

Of course, there are cultural impacts that endure more than two generations. There are millions of third- and fourth-generation Americans who identify themselves as Irish, Italian, Greek, and Polish. To get at that, one might ask:

Example B.17: Most people in this country think of themselves as Americans. However, in addition, is there a particular nationality or ethnic group to which you think of yourself as belonging?

Many people in the United States have lost any sense of pre-American identity, so there will be many "no answers." Moreover, it is obvious that such a question opens the identity gate widely, so a great variety of results can emerge. However, if the goal is to find a cultural heritage of which respondents are aware that is not evident from a person's race, country of birth, and parents' country of birth, that question should find it.

Appendix C:
About Open-Ended Questions

Thirty or forty years ago, as many as half the questions in a standard survey instrument would be open-ended; that is, they would be the type that respondents answered questions in their own words. In the 1990s, however, the open-ended question is becoming increasingly rare. In part, this trend is because many of the measurement goals of survey research can be better achieved when respondents are asked to choose from among a set of answers or to put an answer on a rating scale. In part, as data collection becomes increasingly computerized, interviewers record answers by entering them into a computer, and the survey process goes more smoothly if most answers can be recorded by entering a number rather than a narrative answer.

The open-ended question was discussed to some extent in Chapter 3. As noted there, if the task is to produce an ordered set of answers, or to put answers on a rating scale of some sort, open-ended questions will not do. Moreover, Schuman and Presser (1981) found that even for questions such as, "What is the most important problem?," for which either open or fixed-response strategies will work, providing people with a list of answers to choose from provides more reliable, more interpretable, and possibly more valid responses than the open-ended format.

Nonetheless, there is a role for open-ended questions in survey research. In this appendix, it seemed valuable to briefly go over when such questions might be most appropriate.

The first, and most obvious, situation is when the range of possible answers greatly exceeds what reasonably could be provided. For example, if people are asked to choose their favorite entertainer, their favorite food, or their favorite song, the question must be open-ended; the possible answers clearly would be numerous, diverse, and unanticipatable.

Second, there are some questions that should be answered in a narrative form because the answers are virtually impossible to reduce to a few words. For example, in order to reliably code occupation, respondents need to describe "what kind of work they do on their jobs." Answers consisting of only a word or two often are ambiguous and do not provide enough information to permit coding. Having people answer in their own words, so they can describe what they do, is the way to acquire the information needed. Similarly, to learn about the kind of health problem or condition that led a person to go to a doctor, answers should be in narrative form. Some conditions can be labeled with a single word or two, but in many cases the best answer will require a more descriptive response.

Third, as discussed in Chapter 3, asking open-ended questions is among the best ways to measure knowledge. When knowledge is measured in a true/false or multiple-choice format, some correct answers can occur by chance and not reflect knowledge of the subject. Open-ended answers to questions usually are a better way to find out what people know.

Fourth, when the reasoning behind a conclusion, a behavior, or a preference is of interest, the best way to learn about it is to hear the respondent's own words. Narrative answers about why people do things or the basis on which they have preferences are subject to some unreliability because of differences in respondents' verbal skills and styles. On the other hand, narrative answers give researchers a much more direct window into what people are thinking. If a researcher wants to understand why voters prefer Candidate A to Candidate B or what they do or do not like about their schools, there are many reasons to want to hear narrative answers in addition to, if not instead of, the responses to standardized, fixed-response questions.

Finally, sometimes asking an open-ended question can be the simplest way to gather systematic information about a potentially complicated situation. For example, suppose the goal was to find out how a person came to be homeless. There are numerous possibilities, such as having a house burn down, losing a job, or being thrown out of the house by parents or other family members. However, the diversity of the possible answers, and the potential complexity of some of the scenarios, makes a series of fixed response questions artificial, cumbersome, and not very effective communication. The best approach might be to begin by asking respondents to explain in their own words how they came to be homeless. Once the situation has been explained, respondents can be asked some standard, fixed-response questions to clarify details that are appropriate to the particular situation described by respondents. Such an approach will make the interview interaction much more sensible, at the same time providing the researcher with better, more appropriate information about the actual events.

Answers in narrative form produce data that researchers sometimes find hard to work with. In particular, answers must be coded; someone must read the answers and put them into meaningful numerical categories. The diversity and complexity of answers that can result can make analysis less straightforward than when respondents answer in more structured forms. On the other hand, the result can be a better reflection of what respondents have to say.

Traditionally, when respondents answer in narrative form, coding is separate from data collection. When it is not possible to anticipate exactly what kinds of answers people will give, or how they will phrase them, considerable care can be required to set up a set of standardized coding rules that consistently classify answers into meaningful categories. When this is done appropriately, the rules and policies for classification are refined as the coding process progresses, exceptions are identified and resolved, and coding decisions are check-coded to make sure that they are being made in a consistent way.

When respondents answer questions in a fixed-response format, the answers essentially have already been turned into numerical form, ready for processing. When interviewers enter answers into a computer, the answers are ready for processing; when interviewers are using paper-and-pencil forms, the answers are ready for data entry without a further step. In that context, it is very tempting to have interviewers code answers given in open-ended or narrative form into categories during the interview, rather than introducing a separate coding step.

When the range of answers is quite predictable, the number of possible answers is small, and the rules for classifying answers are relatively simple, it may be appropriate to have interviewers do this kind of coding. For example, it is not uncommon to ask respondents to report level of education in an open-ended way, then have interviewers classify the answers into an ordered set of categories. However, if the classification scheme is at all ambiguous, having interviewers do coding is probably a mistake. Interviewers have a lot to do without having to deal with coding. Moreover, the coding scheme cannot be adapted and refined throughout the data collection process, and none of the coding that interviewers do can be check-coded. Hence, it is not possible to know whether or not they are following consistent procedures for coding, nor is it possible to train them to be better at their coding task. Finally, in studies of interviewer behavior, when questions are asked in open-ended form to be coded into specific categories, interviewers are likely to probe directively in order to ease the classification process (Fowler & Mangione, 1990).

If the structure of the answers is quite clear and the classification system easy, having interviewers classify answers may be all right. However, for most of the interesting and useful things that can be done with narrative answers, their use also requires a separate coding operation to make sure the results that emerge are reliable and valid reflections of what respondents actually say.

Finally, it is worth repeating a theme that recurs in this book: It is critical to specify as clearly as possible in the question what constitutes an adequate answer. This admonition applies particularly to open-ended questions for three reasons.

1. Questions that do not clearly define the response task adversely affect interviewing (Fowler & Mangione, 1990).
2. Variability in understanding the response task is a needless source of variation (and measurement error) among respondents.
3. Diversity of answers stemming from differences in perceptions of how to answer the questions increases the heterogeneity of answers and reduces their analytic value.

Properly designed and coded, questions that are answered in narrative form can be important contributors to good surveys. Knowing when and how to use such questions effectively is one key aspect of being skilled at the design of survey questions.

Appendix D:
Achieving Standardized Interviews

A premise of question design as articulated in this book and a premise of survey measurement in general is that respondents should all answer the same questions, asked exactly as worded. When data collection is self-administered, that simply means that researchers should try to design questions that everybody can read and understand. However, when survey instruments are interviewer administered, there is another dimension to the problem. Schaeffer (1991), Suchman and Jordan (1990), and a compendium of papers compiled by Tanur (1991) have analyzed what actually goes on in survey interviews. They find that in some, if not most, interviews the question-and-answer process is not as standardized as researchers would like to think and as textbooks imply. Their studies suggest the possible value of giving interviewers more flexibility in how they ask questions and how questions are worded so that they are more individualized and tailored to the particular situation of the respondent.

The origins of these thoughts are very real and constitute major challenges to those who design survey instruments. One real problem is that an interview schedule is in fact a protocol for an interaction between two people. It is an interaction very different from what most people are used to. Answering a set of questions asked exactly as worded, frequently by choosing one of a set of answers provided by the interviewer, is not a common kind of interaction. Moreover, respondents will vary significantly in the vocabulary with which they feel comfortable, as well as the situations and feelings that they have to describe. All of these are challenges to standardization that a good survey instrument must be designed to meet.

The idea of having interviewers be flexible in how they word questions and how they administer a survey constitutes a major threat to standardized measurement. As has been discussed throughout the book, we know that small changes in the wording of questions can have big effects on the answers. Particularly in the area of measuring subjective states, it is very difficult to see how reliable measurement could result if interviewers were given more flexibility in the way they ask questions.

When interviewers are trying to gather factual information, there may be more room for innovation in the way question series are structured. Although the wording of questions about objective facts can affect the results, the main issue is whether all respondents have the same perceptions of what to report. There may be ways of ensuring that definitions and expectations are shared, without saddling interviewers with the kind of rigid question formats that typify survey instruments. However, in general, rather than giving interviewers flexibility in how they ask questions, a better approach is to work harder on designing survey instruments that fit the realities of the interaction process. When interviewers and respondents have a difficult time carrying out a standardized interview, it usually is due to poor survey instrument design. The following are some key steps that will help ensure that a survey instrument is a good protocol for a standardized interview process.

1. Provide good definitions of all critical terms. One of the most frustrating and distracting elements in a standardized survey interview is when respondents ask interviewers about the meaning of questions, and all the interviewer can say is, "Whatever it means to you." There are times when it is appropriate to let respondents define terms for themselves. However, for the most part, respondents should be given good definitions of what the questions mean.
2. Questions should be tested in advance to make sure that they can be easily read by interviewers and easily understood the first time by respondents (see Chapter 5).
3. Question series should be structured so that respondents do not routinely answer questions before they are asked. In part, this means having a realistic understanding of how people answer the questions that are posed.

Example D.1: Have you been a victim of a crime in the last year?

Example D.2: (IF YES), What kind of crime was committed against you?

Example D.3: Were you the victim of any other crime in the last year?

Comment: Nine respondents out of ten will answer the first question by saying, "Yes, my car was stolen last year" (or whatever the crime was). When a respondent answers like that, the interviewer is left looking at question D.2 and wondering whether or not to ask it. Question D.2 has already been answered. By the rules of standardization, the interviewer ought to ask D.2. However, by the rules of normal human discourse, asking D.2 is redundant. There will be times, inevitably, when interviewers will appropriately have to ask questions of respondents that they feel respondents have already answered. However, survey instruments can be designed to minimize the extent to which interviewers are put in this situation.

Example D.4: In the past year, have you been the victim of any crime? (What kind of crime is that?) (Any others?)

Comment: This series is identical to the one above, except that interviewers are given discretion about whether or not they have to ask the probes in order to get the information. This kind of flexibility does not undermine the principle of standardization. It does give interviewers the flexibility to adjust the probes to the reality of the answers, without creating an awkward interaction. This simplified approach to the protocol simply is better survey design.

Example D.5: We are interested in why people contribute to the United Way. I am going to read you some of the reasons that people contribute to the United Way, and I would like you to tell me whether these are reasons why you contribute to the United Way. First,...

a. Because the United Way helps many different charities.

Respondent: I give to the United Way because the business where I work has a strong working relationship with the United Way and they strongly encourage all the employees to give.

Interviewer: I see. Let me read that to you again. Because the United Way helps many different charities.

Comment: This is a prototype of an interaction that drives interviewers, respondents, and critics of survey research to distraction. This respondent has one, clear reason for giving to the United Way. The respondent is able to say what the reason is, articulates it well, and has answered the intent of the question. However, the question is designed in a way that does not fit the respondent's answer at all. If the interviewer follows instructions, the interviewer will ask the respondent a series of reasons for giving to the United Way that will seem irrelevant to the respondent and will lead to an awkward interaction. This is the kind of problem that researchers can avoid if they will attend to designing survey instruments in a way that fits the realities of what respondents have to report. There are several approaches to avoiding this problem.

The first, and perhaps easiest, approach is to ask respondents to answer the question in narrative form. Asking people to report on causality or reasons has some inherent unreliability. However, the problems with the way people diagnose causality are present whether the question is in closed or open form. With a variety of answers possible in this situation, the narrative form will likely provide for a better interaction between interviewer and respondent.

Second, reconceptualizing the question can help.

Example D.6: Is the fact that the United Way supports many charities something that you value a lot, some, only a little, or not at all?

Comment: If the question is turned around this way, there are two great benefits. First, it avoids the double-barreled question. In the previous example, respondents were essentially asked both whether or not they value the idea of giving to multiple charities and if that was a reason they gave to United Way.

Those are not necessarily linked. Asking about the perception of the value, and skipping the issue of the diagnosis of its causal role, is probably better conceptual survey design. Second, even after respondents have answered "why" they give to the United Way, they can answer questions about their perceptions of the United Way. These answers can then be correlated with people's propensity to give to the United Way, a better way of tackling the problem of the association between perceptions and behavior than asking people to attribute causality.

If researchers are attentive to how their question design will affect the interaction between respondents and interviewers, they can design questions that will work better from all points of view. Through careful testing such as described in Chapter 5, particularly behavior coding, problems like this can be anticipated and solved in the question design process.

Finally, it is important to train the interviewers to train respondents. Fowler and Mangione (1990) discuss at considerable length the importance of having interviewers teach respondents about standardized data collection. If it is explained to respondents why questions are going to be asked exactly as worded and that they are going to answer in a particular form, they will do a better job of playing their roles in a standardized interaction. Much of the difficulty with standardized interviewing is a failure of respondents to understand the character of a survey interview and what they are expected to do.

Making sure that interviewers are sensitive to the need to train respondents is a critical part of having a good standardized interview. Nonetheless, that can go only so far. The main responsibility should rest with the researcher to design a survey instrument that not only meets standards for good questions, taken one at a time, but also constitutes a good protocol for a standardized interaction between interviewers and respondents.

References

Abrams, D. B., Follick, M. J., Biener, L., Carey, K. B., & Hitti, J. (1987). Saliva cotinine as a measure of smoking status in field settings. *American Journal of Public Health, 77*(7), 846-848.

Anderson, B., Silver, B., & Abramson, P. (1988). The effects of race of the interviewer on measures of electoral participation by blacks. *Public Opinion Quarterly, 52*(1), 53-83.

Andrews, F. M. (1984). Construct validity and error components of survey measures: A structural modelling approach. *Public Opinion Quarterly, 48*(2), 409-422.

Andrews, F. M., & Withey, S. B. (1976). *Social indicators of well-being.* New York: Plenum.

Aquilino, W. S., & Losciuto, L. A. (1990). Effects of interview on self-reported drug use. *Public Opinion Quarterly, 54*(3), 362-391.

Belson, W. A. (1981). *The design and understanding of survey questions.* London, UK: Gower.

Benowitz, N. L. (1983). The use of biological fluid samples in assessing tobacco smoke consumption. In J. Gabrowski & C. S. Bell (Eds.), *Measurement in the analysis and treatment of smoking behavior* (NIDA Research Monograph 48). Rockville, MD: Department of Health and Human Services.

Berk, M., Horgan, C., & Meysers, S. (1982). *The reporting of stigmatizing health conditions: A comparison of proxy and self-reporting.* Hyattsville, MD: National Center for Health Services Research.

Bishop, G. F., Hippler, H.-J., Schwartz, N., & Strack, F. (1988). A comparison of response effects in self-administered and telephone surveys. In R. M. Groves, P. Biemer, L. Lyberg, J. Massey, W. Nicholls, & J. Waksberg (Eds.), *Telephone survey methodology* (pp. 321-340). New York: John Wiley.

Blair, E., & Burton, S. (1987). Cognitive process used by survey respondents in answering behavioral frequency questions. *Journal of Consumer Research, 14,* 280-288.

Bradburn, N. M., Sudman, S., & associates. (1979). *Improving interview method and questionnaire design.* San Francisco: Jossey-Bass.

Cannell, C. F., Groves, R. M., Magilavy, L., Mathiowetz, N. A., & Miller, P. V. (1987). An experimental comparison of telephone and personal health interview studies. *Vital and Health Statistics* (Series 2, No. 106). Washington, DC: Government Printing Office.

Cannell, C. F., Fisher, G., & Bakker, T. (1965). Reporting of hospitalization in the Health Interview Survey. *Vital and Health Statistics* (Series 2, No. 6). Washington, DC: Government Printing Office.

Cannell, C., & Fowler, F. (1965). Comparison of hospitalization reporting in three survey procedures. *Vital and Health Statistics* (Series 2, No. 8). Washington DC: Government Printing Office.

Cannell, C. F., & Marquis, K. H. (1972). Reporting of health events in household interviews: Effects of reinforcement, question length and reinterviews. *Vital and Health Statistics* (Series 2, No. 45). Washington, DC: Government Printing Office.

Cannell, C., Marquis, K., & Laurent, A. (1977). A summary of studies. *Vital and Health Statistics* (Series 2, No. 69). Washington, DC: Government Printing Office.

Cannell, C. F., Miller, P. V., & Oksenberg, L. (1981). Research on interviewing techniques. In S. Leinhardt (Ed.), *Sociological Methodology* (pp. 389-437). San Francisco: Jossey-Bass.

Cannell, C., Oksenberg, L., & Converse, J. (1977). *Experiments in interviewing techniques: Field experiments in health reporting: 1971-1977.* Hyattsville, MD: National Center for Health Services Research.

Clarridge, B. R., & Massagli, M. P. (1989). The use of female spouse proxies in common symptom reporting. *Medical Care, 27*(4), 352-366.

Converse, J. M., & Presser, S. (1986). *Survey questions: Handcrafting the standardized questionnaire.* Beverly Hills, CA: Sage.

Cronbach, L. (1951). Coefficient alpha and the internal structure of tests. *Psychiatrika, 16,* 297-334.

Cronbach, L., & Meehl, P. (1955). Construct validity in psychological tests. *Psychological Bulletin,* 281-302.

Densen, P., Shapiro, S., & Balamuth, E. (1963). Health interview responses compared with medical records. *Vital and Health Statistics* (Series 2, No. 7). Washington, DC: Government Printing Office.

DeVellis, R. F. (1991). *Scale development: Theory and applications.* Newbury Park, CA: Sage.

Dillman, D. A., & Tarnai, J. (1991). Mode effects of cognitively designed recall questions: A comparison of answers to telephone and mail surveys. In P. N. Biemer, R. M. Groves, L. E. Lyberg, N. A. Mathiowetz, & S. Sudman (Eds.), *Measurement errors in surveys* (pp. 367-393). New York: John Wiley.

Droitcour, J., Caspar, R. A., Hubbard, M. L., et al. (1991). The item count technique as a method of indirect questioning: A review of its development and a case study application. In P. N. Biemer, R. M. Groves, L. E. Lyberg, N. A. Mathiowetz, & S. Sudman (Eds.), *Measurement errors in surveys* (pp. 185-210). New York: John Wiley.

Eisenhower, D., Mathiowetz, N. A., & Morganstein, D. (1991). Recall error: Sources and bias reduction techniques. In P. N. Biemer, R. M. Groves, L. E. Lyberg, N. A. Mathiowetz, & S. Sudman (Eds.), *Measurement errors in surveys* (pp. 367-393). New York: John Wiley.

Forsyth, B. H., & Lessler, J. T. (1991). Cognitive laboratory methods: A taxonomy. In P. N. Biemer, R. M. Groves, L. E. Lyberg, N. A. Mathiowetz, & S. Sudman (Eds.), *Measurement errors in surveys* (pp. 393-418). New York: John Wiley.

Fowler, F. J. (1992). How unclear terms affect survey data. *Public Opinion Quarterly, 56*(2), 218-231.

Fowler, F. J., Jr. (1993). *Survey research methods* (2nd ed.). Newbury Park, CA: Sage.

Fowler, F. J., & Mangione, T. W. (1990). *Standardized survey interviewing.* Newbury Park, CA: Sage.

Fox, J. A., & Tracy, P. E. (1986). *Randomized response: A method for sensitive surveys.* Newbury Park, CA: Sage.

Greenberg, B., Abdel-Latif, A., & Simmons, W. H. D. (1969). The unrelated question randomized response model: Theoretical framework. *Journal of the American Statistical Association, 64*(326), 520-539.

Groves, R. M. (1989). *Survey errors and survey costs.* New York: John Wiley.

Hauser, R. M., & Massagli, M. P. (1983). Some models of agreement and disagreement in repeated measurments of occupation. *Demography, 20*(4), 449.

Horvitz, D., & Lessler, J. (1978). Discussion of total survey design. *Health Survey Methods: Second Biennial Conference* (DPHEW Publication No. PHS 79-3207, pp. 43-47). Hyattsville, MD: National Center for Health Services Research.

Hsiao, W., Braun, P., Dunn, D. L., Becker, E. R., Douwe, Y., Verrilli, D. K., Stamenovic, E., & Shiao-Ping, C. (1992). An overview of the development and refinement of the resource-based relative value scale. *Medical Care, 30*(11, Nov. supplement), NS1-NS12.

Jabine, T. B. (1987). Reporting chronic conditions in the National Health Interview Survey: A review of tendencies from evaluation studies and methodological test. *Vital and Health Statistics* (Series 2, No. 105, DHHS Pub. No. PHS 87-1397). Washington, DC: Government Printing Office.

Jabine, T. B., Straf, M. L., & Tanur, J. M. (1984). *Cognitive aspects of survey methodology: Building a bridge between disciplines.* Washington, DC: National Academic Press.

Kallick-Kaufmann, M. (1979). The micro and macro dimensions of gambling in the United States. *The Journal of Social Issues, 35*(3), 7-26.

Krueger, R. A. (1988). *Focus groups.* Newbury Park: Sage.

Kulka, R. A., Schlenger, W. E., Fairbank, J. A., Jordan, K., Hough, R. L., Marmar, C. R., & Weiss, D. S. (1989). Validating questions against clinical evaluations: A recent example using diagnostic interview schedule-based and other measures of Post-Traumatic Stress Disorder. In F. J. Fowler, Jr. (Ed.), *Conference Proceedings of Health Survey Research Methods* (DHHS Pub. No. PHS 89-3447, pp. 27-34). Washington, DC: National Center for Health Services Research.

Lehnen, R. G., & Skogan, W. G. (1981, December). *Current and historical perspectives.* (The National Crime Survey Working Papers, Vol I). Washington, DC: Department of Justice, Bureau of Justice Statistics.

Lessler, J., & Tourangeau, R. (1989, May). Questionnaire design in the cognitive research laboratory. *Vital and Health Statistics* (Series 6, No. 1). Washington, DC: Government Printing Office.

Lessler, J. T. (1987). *Use of laboratory methods and cognitive science for the design and testing of questionnaires.* Stockholm: Statistics Sweden.

Locander, W., Sudman, S., & Bradburn, N. (1976). An investigation of interview method, threat and response distortion. *Journal of the American Statistical Association, 71*(354), 269-275.

Loftus, E. F., Smith, K. D., Klinger, M. R., & Fiedler, J. (1991). Memory and mismemory for health events. In J. Tanur (Ed.), *Questions about questions: Inquiries into the cognitive basis of surveys* (pp. 102-137). New York: Russell Sage Foundation.

Madow, W. (1967). Interview data on chronic conditions compared with information derived from medical records. *Vital and Health Statistics* (Series 2, No. 23). Washington, DC: Government Printing Office.

Mangione, T., Hingson, R., & Barret, J. (1982). Collecting sensitive data: A comparison of three survey strategies. *Sociological Methods and Research, 10*(3), 337-346.

Mangione, T. W., Fowler, F. J., Jr., & Louis, T. A. (1992). Question characteristics and interviewer effects. *Journal of Official Statistics, 8*(3), 293-307.

Marquis, K. (1978). *Record check validity of survey responses: A reassessment of bias in reports of hospitalization.* Santa Monica, CA: RAND.

Martin, E., DeMaio, T. J., & Campanelli, P. C. (1990). Context effects for census measures of race and Hispanic origin. *Public Opinion Quarterly, 54*, 551-566.

McDowell, I., & Newell, C. (1987). *Measuring health: A guide to rating scales and questionnaires.* New York: Oxford University Press.

Moore, J. C. (1988). Self/proxy response status and survey response quality. *Journal of Official Statistics, 4*(2), 155-172.

Morgan, D. C. (1988). *Focus groups as qualitative research.* Newbury Park, CA: Sage.

Morton-Williams, J., & Sykes, W. (1984). The use of interaction coding and follow-up interviews to investigate comprehension of survey questions. *Journal of the Market Research Society, 26,* 109-127.

Neter, J., & Waksberg, J. (1964). A study of response errors in expenditure data from household interviews. *Journal of the American Statistical Association, 59,* 18-55.

Nunnally, J. C. (1978). *Psychometric theory.* New York: McGraw-Hill.

Oksenberg, L., Cannell, C. F., & Kalton, G. (1991). New strategies for testing survey questions. *Journal of Official Statistics, 7,* 349-365.

Parry, H., & Crossley, H. (1950). Validity of responses to survey questions. *Public Opinion Quarterly, 14,* 61-80.

Payne, S. (1951). *The art of asking questions.* Princeton, NJ: Princeton University Press.

Presser, S. (1989). Pretesting: A neglected aspect of survey research. In F. J. Fowler, Jr. (Ed.), *Conference Proceedings of Health Survey Research Methods* (DHHS Pub. No. PHS 89-3447, pp. 35-38). Washington, DC: National Center for Health Services Research.

Rainwater, L. (1974). *What money buys: Inequality and the social meanings of income.* New York: Basic Books.

Rasinski, K. A. (1989). The effect of question wording on public support for government spending. *Public Opinion Quarterly, 53,* 388-394.

Robinson, J. P., Rusk, J. G., & Head, K. B. (1968, September). *Measures of political attitudes* (Library of Congress # 68-65537). Ann Arbor, MI: Survey Research Center, Institute for Social Research.

Robinson, J. P., & Shaver, P. R. (1973). *Measures of social psychological attitudes* (Rev. ed.). Ann Arbor, MI: Survey Research Center, Institute for Social Research.

Robinson, J. P., Shaver, P. R., & Wrightsman, L. S. (Eds.). (1991). *Measures of personality and social psychological attitudes* (Vol. 1). San Diego, CA: Academic Press.

Rodgers, W. L., & Herzog, A. R. (1989). The consequences of accepting proxy respondents on total survey error for elderly populations. In F. J. Fowler, Jr. (Ed.), *Conference Proceedings of Health Survey Research Methods* (DHHS Pub. No. PHS 89-3447, pp. 139-146). Washington, DC: National Center for Health Services Research.

Royston, P. N. (1989). Using intensive interviews to evaluate questions. In F. J. Fowler, Jr. (Ed.), *Conference Proceedings of Health Survey Research Methods* (DHHS Pub. No. PHS 89-3447, pp. 3-8). Washington DC: National Center for Health Services Research.

Schaeffer, N. C. (1991). Interview: Conversation with a purpose or conversation? In P. N. Biemer, R. M. Groves, L. E. Lyberg, N. A. Mathiowetz, & S. Sudman (Eds.), *Measurement errors in surveys* (pp. 367-393). New York: John Wiley.

Schaeffer, N. C., & Bradburn, N. M. (1989). Respondent behavior in magnitude estimation. *Journal of the American Statistical Association, 84*(406), 402-413.

Schuman, H. H., & Presser, S. (1981). *Questions and answers in attitude surveys.* New York: Academic Press.

Schwartz, N., & Hippler, H. (1991). Response alternatives: The impact of their choice and presentation order. In P. N. Biemer, R. M. Groves, L. E. Lyberg, N. A. Mathiowetz, & S. Sudman (Eds.), *Measurement errors in surveys* (pp. 41-56). New York: John Wiley.

Schwarz, N., Knauper, B., Hippler, H.-J., Noelle-Neumann, E., & Clark, L. (1991). Rating scales: Numeric values may change the meaning of scale labels. *Public Opinion Quarterly, 55,* 570-582.

188   IMPROVING SURVEY QUESTIONS

Sieber, J. (1992). *Planning ethically responsible research: Developing an effective protocol.* Newbury Park, CA: Sage.
Smith, A. F. (1991). Cognitive processes in long-term dietary recall. *Vital and Health Statistics* (Series 6, No. 4, Public Health Services). Washington, DC: Government Printing Office.
Smith, T. W. (1991). Context effects in the general social survey. In P. N. Biemer, R. M. Groves, L. E. Lyberg, N. A. Mathiowetz, & S. Sudman (Eds.), *Measurement errors in surveys* (pp. 367-393). New York: John Wiley.
Stewart, A. L., & Ware, J. E., Jr. (Eds.). (1992). *Measuring functioning and well-being: The medical outcomes study approach.* Durham, NC: Duke University Press.
Stewart, D. W., & Shamdasani, P. N. (1990). *Focus groups.* Newbury Park, CA: Sage.
Suchman, L., & Jordan, B. (1990). Interactional troubles in face-to-face survey interviews. *Journal of the American Statistical Association, 85,* 232-241.
Sudman, S., & Bradburn, N. (1974). *Response effects in surveys.* Chicago: Aldine.
Sudman, S., & Bradburn, N. (1982). *Asking questions.* San Francisco: Jossey-Bass.
Sudman, S., & Ferber, R. (1971). A comparison of alternative procedures for collecting consumer expenditure data for frequently purchased items. *Journal of Marketing Research, 11,* 128-135.
Sudman, S., Finn, A., & Lannon, L. (1984). The use of bounded recall procedures in single interviews. *Public Opinion Quarterly, 48,* 520-524.
Tanur, J. (Ed.). (1991). *Questions about questions: Inquiries into the cognitive bases of surveys.* New York: Russell Sage Foundation.
Turner, C. F., Lessler, J. T., & Gfroerer, J. C. (1992). *Survey measurement of drug use: Methodological studies.* Washington, DC: National Institute on Drug Abuse, Department of Health and Human Services.
Turner, C. F., & Martin, E. (Eds.). (1984). *Surveying subjective phenomena.* New York: Russell Sage.
Ware, J. (1987). Standards for validating health measures: Definition and content. *Journal of Chronic Diseases, 40,* 473-480.
Willis, G. B., Royston, P., & Bercini, D. (1989). Problems with survey questions revealed by cognitively-based interviews. *Proceedings, 5th Annual Research Conference* (pp. 345-360). Washington, DC: Bureau of the Census.

Index

About the Author

Floyd J. Fowler, Jr. received his Ph.D. in social psychology from the University of Michigan. He has been a Senior Research Fellow at the Center for Survey Research, University of Massachusetts-Boston since 1971; he was director of the center for 14 years. Dr. Fowler also taught survey methods at the Harvard School of Public Health for 7 years and is currently a research associate of the Dartmouth Medical School. Although he has been actively involved in surveys covering a wide range of subject areas, including crime, health, housing, transportation, government services, and religion, the central focus of his research interests has been on sources of error in survey research. Priorities reflected in his recent work are reducing interviewer-related error and improving the design and evaluation of survey questions.